# *Bread for the Journey*

# Bread for the Journey

## Homilies

Peter Steele SJ

Illustrations by Tim Metherall

DAVID LOVELL PUBLISHING
MELBOURNE AUSTRALIA

First published in 2002 by

David Lovell Publishing
PO Box 44, Kew East
Victoria 3102 Australia
tel/fax +61 3 9859 0000
publisher@davidlovellpublishing.com

© Copyright 2002 Peter Steel SJ

This work is copyright. Apart from any fair dealing for the purposes of private study, research, criticism or review, as permitted under the Copyright Act, no part may be reproduced by any process without written permission. Inquiries should be addressed to the publisher.

Illustarations by Tim Metherall.
Typeset in 11.5/14 Perpetua
This edition printed through Ingram Spark

National Library of Australia Cataloguing-in-Publication data

Steele, Peter, 1937 - 2012.

   Bread for the journey : homilies

   Includes index.
   ISBN 978 1 86355 083 3.

   1. CatholicChurch – Sermons. Sermons Austrtalian.
   I. Title

252.02

# Contents

Introduction   ix

**TIMES**
Irony as Virtue, Cynicism as Vice   3
Roadworkers   7
Light of the World   10
Rejoice Always   13
Promises Made Good   16
Long Haul, Good Taste, Retrieval   18
Baptizing the Lord   21
Burning Bush   24
Six Oases in the Desert   27
Four Abrahams   30
*Christus Aquarius*   33
Perishing   35
The Expectation of Heaven   37
Christ the Palmer   40
Making the Crooked Straight   43
Magnolias   45
Twinned with Thomas   48
At the End of the Day   50
Christ as Misfit, as Venturer, as Way   53
The Mind's Guests   56
Keep in Touch   60
Crowd and Community   63
Threefold Love   66
The Embodiment of God   69
Hill and Valley   73
The Shepherd on the Cross   76
Blessings in Disguise   79
Lord of the Motley Array   82

SEASONS
The Lord of Autumn   87
Power, Love, Wisdom   90
Blessed Australia   94
Anzac Day and Easter   97
The Self at Play   99
The Run   103
God's Comfort   106
Halloween   109
The Man With the Fish and the Bread   112
Earthquakes, et cetera   116
Goodbye and Hello   118

PEOPLE
Hospitality of the Heart   125
An Original   128
Past Master   132
Not the Prime Minister   135
Shifts of the Spirit   139

PLACES
Grass, Squirrel, Christ   147
Friends Marrying   151
Home   154
The Salmon of Wisdom   156
The Wild Prayer of Longing   160
The Light of Wisdom   163
A Raising Spirit   166
The Confused and the Evil   169
The Wars of Love   171
On Taking Experience Seriously   174
Praying in a Certain Place   177
Roads and Lodgings   180
She'll Be Right   183
Need and Gratitude   186
Day and Hour   189

At the Tip of Our Tongue    191
Angels and Others    194
The Ointment and the Vinegar    198

STORIES
Good Samaritans    203
Of Love and Waste    206
Taking Away the Sins of the World    209
Our Father    212
Outsiders    214
Providence and Pressure    219
The Abraham Within    222
Like Sheep    225
Gambles    228
If I Am the One, Let These Others Go    231

CREED
We Believe …    237
One God, the Father Almighty    240
Maker of Heaven and Earth    243
Jesus Christ, His Only Son, Our Lord    246
For Our Salvation, Came Down from Heaven    249
On Saying Yes    251
For Our Sake, Crucified Under Pontius Pilate    254
And Buried    257
He Rose    260
Ascended to the Right Hand of the Father    263
To Judge the Living and the Dead    266
The Holy Ghost: Intimate and Ultimate    269
Lane and Planet: Believing in the Church    272
Standing Up Once and For All    274

Indexes    277

# *Introduction*

IN A FAMOUS PASSAGE SHAKESPEARE REFERS TO 'sermons in stones'. Many writers before him had adopted the same idea, namely that the world itself is a God-given volume, there for our reading. The notion is rejected by many, whether scornfully or with regret, but I welcome it and believe it to be true. As a Jesuit, I have been schooled in a tradition which urges constant attention to traces of divine presence in our wounded human world. And as someone who has for the last forty years been a participant in the life of a secular university, I am aware of scepticism about any such attitude. No doubt these homilies are coloured by both of these circumstances.

They are certainly coloured by an awareness that it is the homilist's business to break a bread which he has not made: 'Thy word is all, if we could spell' wrote George Herbert, the seventeenth-century Anglican priest and poet. The homilies that follow are indeed attempts to spell out some of what God is saying to us, whether in the world shared by all, or in the 'book', the Bible, held out by us by the church.

The context of each of these 'spellings' is a Mass, that thanksgiving ceremony which is always in season. Most of the homilies were delivered at Newman College, at the University of Melbourne, and a few in the chapel at Georgetown University, in Washington DC. In both cases the congregation was various, and I hope that what was said was determined more by Christian and Catholic considerations at large than by too-localized concerns. At the same time, I should like to record my gratitude to those who, by their attendance at the Masses, occasioned the writing.

In the end the words are of little or no consequence compared with the Word. But the whole of Christianity hinges on the proposition that God can turn trivial things to his own powerful and merciful purpose. It is my hope and prayer that, sometimes, here too it may be so.

Peter Steele SJ

# TIMES

ADVENT

# *Irony as Virtue, Cynicism as Vice*

### 1st Sunday of Advent, Year A

HERE COMES ADVENT AGAIN, AND SOME OF US will notice, ruefully, how quickly it has happened. It's not that we haven't been busy with this, that and the other since last time round: and it's not that we haven't been in the midst of events of one kind or another, bitter and sweet. Many of us will have been to weddings, and to funerals, those festivals of waxing life and waning life. Most of us will have sensed something wedding-like, something funeral-like, in our own personal and private fortunes, whatever has been going on in public.

These experiences are, as it were, the yield from our gazing into life's mirror. Nobody, man or woman, ever looks into a mirror without an element of enquiry about good news or bad news—mirrors really are formidable things, even if they cost us only ninety-nine cents each. You look at yours, I look at mine, and we find that much has indeed been happening, in the midst of our customary pragmatic business. Advent invites us to make a longer halt than usual in front of the mirror, and to enquire how things stand with us now.

Physically reliable mirrors are a quite recent invention: but for thousands of years the Christian church has been gazing into its public, its shared, mirror, which is the Bible. We have just found that Isaiah was saying that, in a day to come, the Lord would so move people that they would 'beat their swords into ploughshares and their spears into pruning hooks; one nation shall not raise the sword against another, nor shall they train for war again.' And when we heard this visionary statement, or when we have read it for ourselves in the Bible, we ought at least sometimes stand still and ask what we make of it. Is it, after all, the religious equivalent of Muzak, something to glide over the eardrums without touching the mind? I went to a circus recently, at which one could have cotton-candy or fairy-floss—a vanishing imitation of food, as the circus itself is a vanishing imitation of life's real events and tasks. Are the Bible's prophetic visions of a world without ferocity so many circus-performances: are its words so much fairy-floss?

These are not rhetorical questions. There are many hundreds of thousands of people in Australia, probably millions, who were, once, exposed with some frequency to God's visionary word, and who now seem to take about as much notice of it as any of us does of the Melbourne telephone directory of 1964. Are we so different from them? I don't see why we should assume that we are. Advent is indeed a season of confrontation, a season to give us pause. It presses upon us the necessity to *be genuine* with God, and with one another, and with ourselves. It urges us to be less smoothly-flowing in our relationships, and in our prayers, and in our constant concessions to ourselves. Advent is a nuisance. Its use is to be a nuisance. Advent has some of the reek of John the Baptist about it, that deeply offensive man. And, in God's providence, without John the Baptist, Jesus the transformer and the vindicator did not come.

So, to come back to Isaiah's visionary talk about an end to hostilities, where do we stand? I would suggest that where we might appropriately stand is on a terrain of some irony but not in the territory of cynicism. Let me explain. Australian culture is rich in ironical visions—in seeing things from more than one perspective, and in having one perspective challenge another. God knows where we got this from: we may have picked it up from the Irish, or from some other untriumphant group: but wherever it came from, it is all over the place in Australia. Personally, I think that this is a great, a providential, gift: it is a resource against obsession, and against tyranny, which is much in its favour. We test visionary claims in stringent

'Advent invites us to make a longer halt
than usual in front of the mirror, and to
enquire how things stand with us now.'

ways, again and again. The bigger the claim, the bigger the test. It is a form of behaviour which fits in very well with our Lord's ironical, testing, form of speech. It is fine. It is Advent talk.

But cynicism, or instinctive scornfulness, does not test anything. It simply goes on being spun forth—like a kind of poisoned cotton-candy, or poisoned fairy-floss. There is nothing *in* cynicism, nothing to it, except a proneness to un-do and dis-able. Faced with Isaiah's visionary claim that (in modern terms) the missiles can be dismantled, the aircraft carriers can be junked, the Kalashnikovs can be recast as hoe and spade, cynicism proceeds to bleed all vitality out of such talk. What cynicism does, on the world stage, or in your nearest barber-shop or office or bar-room or bedroom, is to worship *futility:* In the place of Bethlehem's star, blazing with power and with possibility, it sets a dark zero, a vacuum into which aspiration is sucked and annulled. It is no way for you or me to go. It is no way Christ our Lord could ever go.

*Newman: November 1998*

ADVENT

# *Roadworkers*

## 2nd Sunday of Advent, Year A

SOME YEARS AGO I WAS DRIVING ALONG A winding road in Donegal, in hilly country in Ireland. It was midday, and I paused for lunch in a small pub there. In came a man who had been working on the road outside, and he insisted on buying me a drink. There was no way, as the publican joined him in insisting, that I could be allowed to buy him a drink in return—I was the guest, and he was the host. Now I am sure that I could much better have afforded the hospitality than he could: but he was determined not only to keep the road in good shape, but to smooth my path through his country. He was a good advertisement for Ireland; and he was, at least at that moment, a model Christian.

The Gospel today tells us of John the Baptizer, who was a roadworker for the Lord. Jesus was to call himself 'the Way—the Road': the first Christians said that they were the 'followers of the Way'. John, Jesus' cousin, and a person whom Jesus praised as perhaps he praised nobody else, made it his business to make more feasible the Lord's creative and saving work in the world. John was as rough as bags, as rough as any traditional prophet—he rasped the consciousness, and so the conscience, of anybody who would listen to him. When you are mending roads, you rip them up a good deal before you smooth them out: the smoothing won't be much good without the ripping. John was like that. He assumed that we have, probably too soon, over-smoothed our own lives. When I was a young airforce cadet, marching around on a parade-ground, the ground was called the bullring, and the surface was called bulldust. John thought that we were prone to parade on bulldust a lot of the time, and he thought that we could do better than that.

And so did our Lord, who learned some of his style from his cousin. Both of them asked their contemporaries, and the Lord especially asks us today, whether we cannot improve our ways, whether we cannot take a new way. Christianity is about life-long conversion. There simply are no Christian graduates from the need for conversion—never have been, never will be. This does not mean that what is called for is some form of self-dismissal, let alone some form of self-hatred; our Lord says, 'I have come to bring life, and life on a generous scale': he is the originator and the sponsor of the love of our own blessed selves. But just as we should from time to time put our bodies under some stress, and just as we should every day do some bodily cleansing, and trimming, and regulating, so it should be with the fashion in which, intellectually and emotionally and imaginatively, we pick our way through life.

If I could make you all a gift for Christmas, it would be that you should realize that we are all more free than we suppose. We are freer to be growing persons—path-finders, path-takers, path-stayers—than most people have told us, whether inside the Church or outside it. Sometimes people blandish us; sometimes they manipulate us: sometimes they bluff us, or blackmail us emotionally, or bully us. And it works—for dead-end people who conceive of others as dead-end people too. But what John the rover, and Jesus the rover, brought home to at least a few people—otherwise, we would not be here in this chapel today—is that we *can* take possession of our own lives. We do not have to be diminished by the mean-spiritedness of others. Slavery may be contagious, but so is liberty. The path to both ways forks open in our own hearts.

To go back to my nameless Irish friend in the hills of Ireland, he knew no more of me than I did of him, but fifteen years later he is still a prompter of generosity in me, a roadmaker for my own heart in Australia. I can't buy him a drink today, any more than he would

*Times*

let me do then, but I can invite you all to join in a prayer for him, and for all those dear to him. In the end, all such prayers turn out to be prayers for all of us on our way. They are easily prayed: but let us, in Advent, also remember the need for our ways to be rasped up somewhat before they are made smooth for the future.

*Newman: December, 1992*

ADVENT

# Light of the World
### 3rd Sunday of Advent, Year A

I WAS ONCE IN AN AIRLINER THAT FLEW, AT THIS time of year, over Afghanistan. It was a clear night and there was a full moon—what used to be called, during the Second World War, a bomber's moon. You could look down and see the snow-covered mountains, and very beautiful they were; but you also knew that this was a bomber's moon once more, only this time it was not the British or the Germans who were opening the bomb-bays: it was the Russians who might have their fighter-bombers or their helicopter gunships out, and the Afghans who might have the ground-to-air missiles up and aimed. Down there, if you were close enough, there would be stains on the snow.

I remembered this when I thought about our Gospel for today. At first hearing, we might be disposed to protest. After all, however secularized and commercialized and cynical the public hoop-la of Christmas has become, surely there is much to admire in the gift-buying and the gift-giving; surely, too, after a year's grind at whatever range of things we have been doing, the eating and drinking and making merry is its own justification; and surely, after all the grief-mongering and anxiety-provoking with which the media tends to deluge us, we don't need the Church getting on that dark and rickety bandwagon and providing us with a Gospel all about the ominous and the upsetting. 'Who needs it?', we may feel.

'Get a map of the world, close your eyes,
and put your finger on some land mass,
and the betting is that now or in the recent past
institutionalized violence will have
played its part there.'

## Bread for the Journey

And the answer, my sisters and brothers, is that we do. We need it, need some of it at least, so that we may remember two things: the world that existed at the time of our Lord's first coming, and the world in which we live in expectation of his conclusive coming. It was, after all, the army of the Roman empire, the army trained to use its swords like meat-cleavers, which ensured that Jesus would be born away from home: and it was the army of Herod, a satellite king, which ensured that nameless Jewish children would have a baptism of blood when Jesus was born in Bethlehem. Behind the snowy elegance of every Christmas crib, there loom the dark shadows of life's enemies.

Alas, I do not need to work hard to think of the modern equivalents of these sorry events, and nor do you. Get a map of the world, close your eyes, put your finger on some land-mass, and the betting is that now or in the recent past institutionalized violence will have played its part there. And even if that is not so, I would defy anyone to find any settled spot on earth where animus does not smoulder to some degree. Human angers are pandemic—sometimes latent, sometimes obvious, always a factor. Imaginative writers speak sometimes of life on Mars, and of Martian behaviour: but if Mars was the Roman god of war, a visitor to our planet might think it not Earth but Mars after all.

And that is why the recitative of 'Peace on earth' is so relevant, and so poignant, at this time of the year. Not long ago we celebrated the feast of Christ the King, and when the Preface of that feast was tallying the qualities of a world made good in the end by the power and authority of Christ, the last word in the catalogue was 'peace'. Christmas invites us, indeed summons us, to throw in our lot with that Lord—to become the blessed 'peacemakers' whom he himself called and commended. He found at firsthand how prone our species and society are to angers, and to all the injustices and horrors which flow from them. He can, through the power of his risen Presence, change those lethal energies into forces for good. So let us pray together today for an openness in ourselves to be converted as each one needs conversion: and let us pray for this often-ravaged world, of which Christ the Lord is now a perpetual citizen, and which he loves so well.

*Newman: December, 1995*

ADVENT

# *Rejoice Always*
4th Sunday of Advent, Year B

MY BROTHERS AND SISTERS, TWENTY-NINE YEARS ago to the hour, I celebrated my first Mass as a priest. It was in Perth, in my parents' parish church, and my much younger brother, then still a schoolboy, stood up at the lectern and read out the second reading we have just heard. This is the one in which St Paul, writing to the new Christians in Thessalonika, tells them that he 'wants them to be happy'. I can still hear my brother's fresh young voice saying, as St Paul dictated, 'I will say it again: I want you to be happy.' It was a good word then, and it is a good word now.

Mind you, not everybody, and not every Christian, seems to be convinced that hoping to be happy is of much account. Sometimes this stems from bitter experience, whether public or private. I need not recite for you the long sad tale of notorious suffering in our now-waning century; it is a sickening business, and all the more sickening for its being such public property. And I could not, even if I wanted to, feel my way into those griefs and pains which are distinctive to each of us—the things which are so many honed blades in the darkness of our minds and hearts. Our incentives to unhappiness are rarely hard to recall.

But the fact is that Christianity does not take the obvious way, does not concede without protest to worldly-wisdom, does not go with the social flow. I know that, over the centuries, Christianity has often been coopted by those in power to bless its policies, and its armies, and its prizes, and its self-preenings: I know that Christianity has been wreathed with garlands because it has apparently been, in the contemptible expression, 'at the cutting edge' of something or other. Whenever this takes place—and it is certainly taking place as I speak, in various parts of the world, as it always has taken place—we may appropriately be reminded of our Lord's parable about the blind leading the blind, who, as he assures us, will all fall into some ditch or other. Next time you find somebody speaking well of Christianity in secular society, say some prayers for the Christians, and say some prayers for those who are being nice to them: both lots will need your prayers.

For the fact is that while we Christians do have a title to happiness, as my young brother was right to proclaim, and as St Paul was right to insist, our title to happiness, our *vocation* to happiness, indeed, takes its validity only from our readiness to stump along after our Lord, who is certainly the source and sponsor of all joy, but who is resolute in his readiness to go the frequently-odious path of realism to carry joy through to its vindication.

I cannot tell you along what particular path you must carry the torch of hope for happiness. What I can and do say is that you must not take either of a couple of by-paths. You must not, firstly, take the by-path of glib affirmation—as if all were well with the world at large, or with your personal world. Much is not well with the world at large—that world to which Jesus was committed: we cannot deny this. And some things, at least, are not well with your personal world, or mine: and it is mere whistling in the dark to deny this.

But if the blind lurching of randomly-invoked happiness will not do, neither will the path of cynicism, neither will scorn. I cannot speak for you, but it seems to me that a kind of cocky scornfulness, a kind of implacable cynicism, is often to be found in Christian quarters. It dresses itself up as the God-hauntedness of Christ—the best man's yearning for the best place. All too frequently, though, it is merely one of the devil's seedier accomplishments. If we do not have the heart for happiness, then for God's sake let us not congratulate ourselves upon this. It may be that it is indeed the devil who has knocked the heart out of us.

*Times*

Here we are, today, near enough to Christmas—to Christmas, a feast whose narrative records dislodgement, indifference, perplexity, shock, struggle, anxiety, mistrust, and mess: in short, all the makings of unhappiness. And yet, as we all know, this occasion's motif is still happiness—still, in an old word, 'felicity'. By the time our Lord was born, as the Church's tradition assures us, his mother and his mother's cousin Elizabeth had been gathered into a kind of duet of jubilation—a jubilation which could be rendered almost soundless by later events, but whose note was never lost. To try such a way is the authentic policy of Christianity, a policy which is also a quest. A happy Christmas to you, when it comes; without happiness in one real sense or another, it will not in fact have come at all.

*Newman: December, 1999*

CHRISTMAS

# *Promises Made Good*
## Birth of the Lord

SOME OF US WILL REMEMBER THAT THE OPENING OF St John's Gospel, which we have just heard, used to close the Mass. I don't know how this came about, but I can guess at its appropriateness. After all, when we Catholics left the chapel or the church and turned towards our daily affairs, we could be braced and heartened by the challenge to believe anew that 'the Word was made flesh, and dwelt among us, and we saw his glory.' The immense blessing of the Eucharist, which is God's gift to us of Thanksgiving for all his other gifts—that immense blessing was to be carried out and about in a world which often looked quite without gratitude for anything, let along for everything. So to have St John's reminder that the Son of God, who is also the Meaning of God, is abroad in just this world of ours was a great thing to have in our ears as we bustled off on the day's business.

It was so then, and isn't it so today—and most of all at Christmas, at 'Christ's Mass', the birthday Mass for the Lord himself? In one sense or another all of us are devout, or we would not be here today: but even the devout live every day of their lives in a world where few angels do audible singing, few reverent Magi patrol our streets with gifts. Like everybody else, we have to make such sense as we can of the world's frailties and follies, and often that is not much sense at all. On this day, the usual number of babies will be born, as anonymous and as individual as Jesus himself, but we know that all too many of them will be born into the same vulnerability as surrounded him, those couple of thousand years ago: and we know what anxieties and perplexities will shadow the joy of all too many fathers and mothers at this time. They need, and we need, the testimony of the Church that high religious dreams and visions, old yearnings and cherished prophecies, did indeed blessedly come down to earth when that one child saw the light for the first time, and then was buffered with cloth and straw in order to begin to cope with a new world. And one thing for which we should give thanks in this Mass is for the faith God has seen fit to give us that all this is true: that this Child, one of billions, was the one on whom the universe hinges, and hinges for good: just as that Child, full-grown, could be the mortal in whom, up there on his cross, our salvation and our eternal blessing hinges.

In this world, each of us has his or her particular blessings: and for me, one great blessing has been to find particular words 'become flesh', as it were—to find hints and promises and names come good. In the Gospels, our Lord alerts us to this kind of thing when he renames Simon, 'Peter', and tells that rather ricketty and rocky individual that he will after all be rock-like in the things that matter. I leave you with a very modern example of this. A while ago a remarkable American musician, and poet of sorts, died. His name was Louis Hardin: he was eighty-three years old; and he had been blind since early in life. He was a complex person, often I would guess perturbing to others: he was for some time famous as a street performer in New York; he was an acquaintance or friend of some of the most celebrated musicians of the twentieth century; he died in Germany, where he had lived for many years.

His nickname, or tradename, was 'Moondog'—which means, the kind of dog that bays or howls at the moon. I'd guess that he chose the name because it captures so well both a down-to-earthness—which any four-legged beast displays—and a hankering for things beyond, things bright and divine. Louis Hardin, 'Moondog', wasn't a Christian, but his very name is a homely reminder of God's own meaning, and light, and beauty, as both appealing to us, and coming home to us. Perhaps Moondog is in a position to pray for all of us today, and if he is, he will be wishing us a happy Christmas: as the Church does; and as I do.

*Newman: December 1999*

## Long Haul, Good Taste, Retrieval

**Epiphany**

THE GOSPEL TELLS US THAT THE WISE, OR CANNY, visitors to our Lord's birth brought with them gold, and frankincense, and myrrh. We have all seen these wise visitors represented countless times—in Christmas cribs, on Christmas cards, and probably in many other places. Over the centuries, they have been sorted out: they have been thought of as three in number, they have been given different nations or races, and they have even been given specific names.

The gospel doesn't tell us any of these things. What it does say, or at least imply strongly, is that the 'Magi' were 'wise-men'. The bottom line is that they were wise to come and applaud this particular birth; whatever their sins, follies, prejudices or obsessions, they got this bit right—where God took flesh among us, that was a good spot to which to have recourse. Our days and lives, even the fortunate ones, can have an air of the desert about them: but in that desert, a trampled Bethlehem stable can still be an oasis.

A very brief word, which may be relevant to us, about those 'gifts of the Magi'. The first of these is gold. Gold has many good things to be said for it, but one of the reasons why human beings have for so long made such a fuss about it is that it does not decay. Gold, in saintly paintings ancient and modern, stands for eternity—stands for a condition which endures over all the ups and downs of our lives, all our fears and misgivings and dispiritings and extravagant bouncings-back: gold is, as we say, as good as gold—we can rely on it. And when the wise men bring the infant Jesus some gold in symbolic tribute, they are saluting the durability of God—God of our nights and days, of our childhood and youth and middle age and old age: God who is God for good, as we say: God who is golden, as good as gold: who is God for good, who is golden for good.

The second gift is frankincense—'incense', as we would say. Most of us have had a whiff of this, perhaps at Benediction, perhaps at other times. It is rich, savoury stuff: it has a reek of the royal about it. And so it is meant to have. As we sniff it up, we are meant in a sense to be sniffing up a sense of God's fullness, his abundance. Many of us are so busy that we don't have the leisure to savour the plenitude of God's action in his and our universe. The stars come out every night, as we can see even in the clogged night-sky of Melbourne, but few of us count them or wonder at them; our bodies operate, more or less skilfully, every day, and our minds work, and our hearts respond, and there are prodigious miracles involved in every five minutes' happening of these things in each of us each day, waking or sleeping: but on we go, as if this were not so. I am not trying to agitate misgiving in saying this—what right would I have to do that?—only to remind you, and myself, that God is ceaselessly at work, copious and ingenious, on our behalf, on even the least remarked of days. The 'Magi' gave their name, in effect, to what we call 'magic', in the western world: and God truly is the magicians' Magician, the master of daily magic. And this is one of the things saluted by the rich, haunting tang of incense.

And then there is myrrh. Myrrh is a resin which, in our Lord's time, was used as a substance smeared on the bodies of the dead. The word itself means something like 'bitter', and the smearing-moment must always have been a bitter one. In the gospel story, the point of bringing the myrrh was to acknowledge, and to bless, mortality. 'To bless'—that is the challenge: because when something is merely burnt-out, nobody attempts to preserve or to salute it; nobody kisses a dead match. At the beginning of a book whose words I teach each year, the translator has written a dedication—'To the great dead, who will not die.' Putting myrrh upon the 'great dead' offers the hope that they will not die, totally: and bringing myrrh to the vulnerable, mortal baby Jesus offers the hopeful claim that, even though he will die like the rest of us, he will still be deathless—and, in his case, be deathless in being raised up, and in carrying the rest of us up with him in his wide-flung arms.

These are among the things we celebrate today: that Jesus of Nazareth, like gold, will not wear out, however long the day, or the century, or the millennium; that he is copious, fruitful, and never drained-out; and that although he consents to go our mortal way, he remains the great cup of vitality for all of us. These things, the Church says, the Magi were signaling to us; and that is about as wise as you need to be.

*Newman: January, 2000*

BAPTISM

## *Baptizing the Lord*
### Baptism of the Lord

THIS FEAST HAS TO DO WITH THE BAPTIZING OF our Lord and Saviour. All of us have been to baptisms, if only our own. Some of us have played key parts in baptisms—as parents, as godparents, as providers of the baptismal gown, as organizers of the event, as pourers of the water. On the whole, there are probably not too many mixed feelings about baptisms. Marriages or ordinations can have some grey-ish overtones about them, and people have been known to have their doubts about the wisdom of this example or that. By contrast, a baptism seems, almost self-evidently, to be a good way to go. After all, what it does is to induct the child, or the adult, into the Christian community, and who could quarrel with that? So apart from a bit of understandable whimpering or howling on the part of the little person who is being dowsed with water while still clothed, surely everything should be serene.

Often everything is serene, and that seems a very fair thing, particularly for the infant who has usually not so long ago been in the serenity of the womb. But forgive me if I think of a vivid juxtaposition which was seen in one of the 'Godfather' movies. Perhaps you will remember that, there, the producer sliced back and forth between images of a baby's being baptized while, elsewhere in the same city, other members of the child's family were engaged in murderous warfare with one another. Perhaps the producer had nothing in mind but the vividness of the contrast, the melodramatic contrast between the pouring of water and the shedding of blood. Still, we may turn that contrast to our own purposes here.

In the biblical account, the adult Jesus offers himself for baptism. Just why did he do this? I don't know. Like many of his words and deeds, this one is freighted with mystery, with momentousness, and it would be a foolish commentator, and a glib one, who spoke as though the situation was transparent. But let us think along just one line about that moment. The fact is that to let yourself be baptized is to let yourself be engulphed. Often, and properly, these days, a few drops of water take the place of a tide, but they do stand for that tide: baptism is oceanic in its reference. At this time of the year, the radio broadcasts remind us that a creek, or a river, or a swimming-pool, let alone the ocean, can change in seconds from being our solace to being our destroyer. All substantial bodies of water are like that. Their bright face is the face of refreshment, cleansing, and sustaining: their dark face is the face of something quite unbridled.

We may say that when our Lord came forward and was baptized by John, his cousin, he symbolized the fact that he did indeed trust his Father to be his refresher, his sustainer—and even his cleanser, when we think of the grime and sweat and blood that were to come his way before life's course was done. Giving himself to the water's embrace was a foreshadowing of what he was to say at journey's end—that it was to his Father's hands that he entrusted his whole vital being. But we may also say that, going down into the waters of the Jordan River, in company with so many others, he was also immersing himself in the tainted stream of time—of human event, with all its ambiguity, its mingled beauty and ugliness, its great purities and its great profanations. It was, in other words, as though he joined himself not only with the water flowing over the baby's head in *The Godfather*, but with the blood being shed so murderously by that baby's relatives in another place.

One thing that this Feast of the Baptism of the Lord says to us is that he is here to stay. That he will not desert us. That he will not tire of the role, the act, of being 'God-With-Us', because it is not a role or an act—it is himself. I hope that this particular Sunday, this particular day of the Lord, is a consoled and serene one for you, and for me, and I hope for the best in the week to come: but as the Lord told us, 'in the world you will have trouble'. He also said, immediately, 'But do not be afraid: I have conquered the world.' It is in his fidelity to us, his endorsement of us, his love for us, that he conquers the world. The holy water you may take from the stoup at the door as you leave is a reminder of that.

*Newman: January, 1999*

FOR ASH WEDNESDAY

## *Burning Bush*
### Third Sunday of Lent, Year C

WE ARE GIVEN, IN THE FIRST OF TODAY'S readings, one of the most vividly imagined objects in the whole of the Bible—and indeed perhaps in western literature. The young Moses is out shepherding his father-in-law's flock, and he comes to a mountain sacred to God, whose name is Horeb. And there, to his amazement, he sees a bush which is blazing away, but which is not burned up. He comes nearer to see what on earth is going on, and then God speaks to him. From that moment, the whole history of the Israelites is different: and so, eventually, is yours and mine. Why so? Well, because Moses is told that his people's enslavement by the Egyptians will be broken, with God supplying divine power and direction, and Moses himself supplying the human leadership. And all the time, the bush burns and burns but does not dwindle away.

Ever since that episode, Judaism and Christianity alike have, so to speak, been re-kindled from the burning bush. When you were baptized, somebody held a candle for you, a candle to symbolize the light and the power of God's love. When we come to the culmination of Lent, at the Easter Vigil, in the dead of night, new fires will be lit all over the world, fires which speak mutely of the God of sun and stars, and of Christ the Light of life: and from those fires, candle by candle, Christians will pass on the flame which, for a moment, makes visible God's unquenchable vitality. And in between the moment of baptism and the moment of Easter, here we are, with a couple of candles lit as usual on the altar, as they are at every Mass, to signal that our God is not to be found only in desert places or on sacred mountains, but at every altar, every table, every desk, every counter—and, if you keep your eyes open, every bar.

It is not only in Judaism and in Christianity that the element of fire has been able to speak of life. Ancient pagans in many parts of the world turned to it with fascination: and many contemporary artists, who would decline to be identified as believers, engage in fire-talk, in the pages they write or on the canvas or hardboard where they paint. What all of these people recognize is that fire can be an emblem both of the forces we find within ourselves, and of the powers that play upon us from outside. I will say a word about each of these things, as seen with Christian eyes.

Each of us has an array of vitalities, of energies—what might be called personal fires. Some of these are physical: and without these, not only would we not live, but we would have no successors. I do not need to remind most of the inhabitants of this College that sport, for instance, can be an exhilarating thing, and full of meaning beyond its own immediate moment—something which gets striking expression at Olympic Games, for instance, Games which are very appropriately begun with the kindling of new fire. Some of our energies are more than physical—they are intellectual, or emotional. It is mainly with these in view that the College exists. It is because they are so prized that the place was built, and is kept going, and is intended to have a future. Physical or spiritual, our fires are divinely-given and humanly-welcome.

But we all know that fire has two faces, that it can be a life-giver or a death-dealer. This too is so of any of our gifts, our capacities. The body in all its fine form can be a means of domination, of exhibitionism, of seduction. The mind can be a means of deception, of cruelty, of self-absorption. The emotions can become almost our whole world, happily or unhappily, so that the world's shared reality has hardly any purchase on us. At such times, the fire does after all consume us, and we can become ashen people—as Ash Wednesday warns us we might, and challenges us not to be. Lent, then, can be an occasion for us to ask whether we are the directors of our own fires, or merely the material which, bit by bit, it will eat away.

If we think about such matters, it should never be in a spirit of self-dismissal, much less self-hatred. For the great fire-giver is God himself. At another of the Church's principal festivals, Pentecost, the imagery is one of personal flames being given by God to each person: as if, in Michelangelo's great painting of God's touching life into Adam's fingers, it was fire that ran from one to the other. In the prayers and songs that centre around Pentecost, the Holy Spirit of God, God's breath among us, is spoken of many times as the fire-bearer. And in those prayers and songs we ask that he will help us receive the love and the power which, by nature, he is so eager to share.

Failures and disappointments, moral blunders and outright sins, may dispirit us, and turn us sceptical about the possibility of our flaming up again with divine and human vitality: in fact, that is what those failures, those sins, tend of their nature to do. But let us remember today that, as we began this Mass, like all Masses, with an acknowledgement of the damping down of love through our sins, so in this Mass as in all Masses we will receive from between the candles the Lord of the Burning Bush. 'This is the Lamb of God', the priest will say, 'who takes away the sins of the world: happy are those who are called to his supper.' It was, after all, to a young member of a downcast people that the Lord showed himself in the bush at Horeb. He has things to show us, if we will watch, in Parkville this week.

*Newman: for Ash Wednesday, March, 1995*

LENT

# Six Oases in the Desert
## 1st Sunday of Lent, Year A

ALL RELIGIONS TRY TO MAKE SOME SENSE OF WHAT has been going on in history, and try to understand history as being laden with meaning. Christianity does this: Catholicism does this; we try to do it, in a small way, in this chapel at Newman today. In the Old Testament, the Hebrew Bible, the desert bulks large—which is one thing that can link Australians with the writings of thousands of years ago. Most of us live around the rim of this country, but plenty of us, when we want to become really thoughtful, will at one time or another head into the outback, and perhaps into the desert. The huge, undistracted spaces can help us to have undistracted minds and undistracted hearts.

It says in the Old Testament that a particular God-haunted people hit the desert for forty years. Out of that experience—and what led up to it, and what flowed from it—came Judaism, and Christianity, and ultimately a good deal of the world that we know today. This season of 'Lent', which began last Wednesday, lasts for forty days, and it is a ritual reminder of that desert thoughtfulness and yearning, that desert quest for meaning and love and happiness. What God asks of us in these forty days is that, as much as we can manage, we try to muse a bit on who we are, what we amount to, where we are going, and how we may grow well. The six Sundays in Lent amount to oases in the desert of search—little settlements at which we can pause, and take stock of the trip so far.

## Bread for the Journey

The striking feature of the reading from Genesis today, and from the Gospel, is that people are *challenged*. There are other words for this—'cajoled, seduced, bewitched, beckoned'—but 'challenged' is probably still the best word. Whether it is the story of the man and the woman in the garden, or whether it is the story of the lone Christ hacking it in his solitude, in both cases with the one called 'the devil' at hand—either way, what we are talking about is *challenge*: challenge to integrity, challenge to identity, challenge to readiness to be oneself.

Talk about 'the devil' probably makes little impact on most of us. That may not matter, so long as we understand what his title stands for. There are a couple of Greek words which mean, 'the one who throws something against us', and it is from them that we get the notion of the devil. He is the one who keeps the game up to us, the *challenger*. And whether or not we ever give him a moment's thought, if we want to be responsible adults, free selves, givers and receivers of love, we had better take seriously the fact that we live in a milieu of challenge.

All of you, whether this is your first week at Newman, or whether you have been here for some time, came here under challenge. It was an educational challenge to get to the various tertiary institutions to which you belong; it was a further challenge to get to Newman itself. These things matter, and will continue to matter. There is no reason why the universities should keep you around if you do not work hard intellectually; there is no reason why Newman should keep you around unless you grow intellectually, socially, and as far as one can judge, spiritually. Newman is not a shelter for emotionally retarded adolescents, and the priests charged with running it have better things to do than stay here if that looks like being the way the game is to be played. This college, seventy-five years old this year, has never had a better right to issue challenges to those who make up its community.

The fact that you are here today means that your opportunities are enormous. They are opportunities for personal growth in disciplined understanding of the world and of your own lives—the sort of thing universities have always been for. They are also opportunities to grow in bravery, in generosity of heart, in unselfishness, in truthfulness of spirit. Australians tend to be cynics: but in spite of our cynicism, any realist must acknowledge that you have opportunities for joy in understanding, for enlarged horizons, for the lifted heart, which would be envied by hundreds of millions of people throughout the world, if your present situation could be projected in front of them.

If I were the devil of either the Genesis or the Gospel reading today, and if I were looking for something to do at Newman this week, I would try either of two manoeuvres. I would try to dishearten you, or I would try to trivialize you. Some of you are self-doubting, whether you are so by nature or because of your experience so far. Any hard-headed devil would tell you that you don't amount to much, that you are here on false pretences, that you are and you always will be a small-scale person. That's what a devil would say—the one called, sometimes, 'The Father of Lies'.

And some of you are confident enough, with energy, or money, or reputation, or charm, or intelligence, or good looks, to bet on. Any hard-headed devil would tell you to punt all the way on these things—to be unconfrontable, to be unchangeable, to be your own self-absorbed darling. Such a devil would not mention, of course, that somebody defined him as 'the servant of the servants of themselves'. Whatever your gifts, unless you watch your step, you will go away from this little patch of Parkville both older and slighter than you came here.

If this sounds like bad news, it is not meant to be that. This Sunday is the first of the oases, the first of the seasons of self-possession. As we go on in the eucharist, we will as usual deal in the symbols of vitality and growth—bread for sustenance, wine for joy. Your months and years here can easily be like the bread, and like the wine. But nobody except you can make them be either of those things.

*Newman: February, 1993*

LENT

# Four Abrahams

## 2nd Sunday of Lent, Year A

As you will remember, the first words in the Book of Genesis are, 'In the beginning, God created the heavens and the earth.' That has to do with the cosmos; but our first reading today, from that same Book, might also have begun with the words, 'In the beginning', since the calling of Abraham is in effect the beginning of something like history we can understand in modern terms.

At that moment, God both summons Abraham, and all his descendants, and blesses them all. A blessing is always an endorsement. It is an underwriting of who one is, a vindication of one's intimate being. This is what we acknowledge in our own lives when, for instance, as we say, we 'bless ourselves' before grace or at the beginning of the Mass: we trace on our bodies and in our consciousness both the names of our creating God and the memory of our loving Saviour. But, very often, blessings are also summonings—are callings beyond our status quo, are invitations to growth.

So it was with Abraham. We are reminded elsewhere in the Bible that when Abraham did move out from his country and his familiar relationships, he did not know where he was going. He did this not because he was footloose, or crazed, but because it was indeed God who provoked him and called him. And out of that readiness to listen, and that readiness to march, as it were, in the dark, there unfolded the religious history of the Jews, and the coming of Christ, and our very being here in this chapel today.

*Times*

That was long ago, and far away. Abraham could not speak a word of English, partly because there wasn't a word of English for him to speak—the very language came later. And Abraham would not know what a telephone was for, or a modern broom, or the fork on your table. But in spite of those gaps, he was essentially where all of us are many times in our own lives. Because we too are blessed, thousands of times, and we are summoned, thousands of times.

To suggest how this is so, let me name three other, much more recent, Abrahams. Each of them was called to respond to what I call a cry—a cry from the others, or a cry from oneself, or a cry from God. My first Abraham is Abraham Lincoln. I am not trying to paint him, or either of the others, as a saint, which is after all God's business, not mine. He was not universally admired: the London *Times* called him 'the Baboon'. But nobody could deny that, in all the density and complexity of history, Abraham Lincoln, as President of his savagely divided country, had to respond to the cry of his people. There may be times when people in positions of leadership can coast along, but his was not one of those times. For Lincoln, it was a devil of a business to lead his country. When the Civil War came, Lincoln's wife had three brothers who fought for the opposing Southern armies: Lincoln offered the command of the Northern armies to Robert E. Lee, who instead took command of the South. And there were countless other ambiguities and disconcertments. He could no more foretell the future than any of us can: but he was still, genuinely, an 'abrahamic' person in his responding to the cry of 'the others'. This week, somebody, somewhere, will surely offer us just such a cry.

My second Abraham is the American psychologist Abraham Maslow. Maslow had plenty of experience of human folly and wickedness, but, blessedly as it seems to me, he declined to give in to the standard melancholy view that the human being, the human self, is either vicious or a pawn of forces, internal and external. Maslow believed that most people have far more creativity—emotional, intellectual and spiritual—than they make use of. It is as if, in my terms, he listened to the cry of the self, the cry of the soul—a cry which is issued not out of greed, or malice, or desolation, but out of hope to grow, hope to flourish, hope to be. I am certain that Maslow was right. I am certain that the God who brought us miraculously to be at all is intent on re-enacting the blessing given to the first Abraham. I am certain that anyone who habitually wishes to daunt us in our journey through life is doing the devil's work. And this week, too, there will be some cry from each of our hearts, a cry against our own timidities, our own harshnesses, our own callousnesses. It will be in God's name that we will listen to such a cry.

Which brings me to my third Abraham—the Jewish religious thinker, Abraham Heschel. There are many books whose titles indicate that we are seekers, searchers, pilgrims, and so forth: but one of Heschel's books is called *God in Search of Man*. Heschel's meaning is that, in the actualities of our lives—in just that dense historical weave which Abraham Lincoln had to deal with, and in just those cries of the heart for growth and flourishing—no one less than God is present, and pressing. Heschel loved to use the phrase, 'human and holy', since he cherished the fact that it is in the flesh and blood of our lived hours that God can come home to us, and we can come home to God.

Heschel had seen more of the bitterness of life at close quarters than most of us, I hope, will do. He left Poland just six weeks before the Nazi invasion: he called himself 'a brand plucked from the fire', and that fire consumed most of his Jewish people. But he went on, for the rest of his life, attesting that God does indeed bless and summon us every day—through the beauty of creation, for which there are no words good enough, and through the undeniable needs of our brothers and sisters, for which there are no words emphatic enough. For Heschel, God was no mere genial sponsor of our equilibrium: as he said, 'if God is not of supreme importance, he is of no importance.'

Our presence in this chapel, at this Eucharist, points in the same direction. We do what we are doing now, as our Lord told us, to remember the Lord. And whether or not we invoke Heschel's memory, and the memory of so many other Abrahams, we are indeed in the same place as they were, and as Jesus himself was: at the heart of God's world, waiting for God's call.

*Newman: February, 1999*

LENT

# *Christus Aquarius*
## 3rd Sunday of Lent, Year A

I DON'T KNOW WHETHER ANY OF YOU GLANCES AT the 'star-sign' columns in the newspapers, or listens to the astrologers who crop up occasionally on radio. If you do, you will have come across the figure of Aquarius. His name means that he is the 'water-carrier' or 'water-bringer'. For us, he is a figure of fiction, like Goldilocks or Mr Micawber: but he has managed to stick in the mind for many hundreds of years. Perhaps this is in part because we all need, so constantly, bringers of water, or of the various fluids which are all elaborated or modified water. The poet W. H. Auden has a poem called 'First Things First', which ends with the line, 'Thousands have lived without love, not one without water', and whatever about the love, he is right about the water. Cut off the water supply, and even the most impregnable of cities is forced to surrender, the most robust of men or women becomes entirely vulnerable.

Today's Gospel celebrates Christ our Aquarius. In the account of his conversation with the woman at Jacob's Well, he wants and needs a drink, but as it emerges, the woman's need is deeper, and his claim is that he can satisfy the thirst that runs all through her. This story is taken from St John's Gospel, which makes much of Christ the food-giver, Christ the drink-bringer. One reason John does this is because he wants to show our Lord to us as the primal figure, the elemental human being and divine being. It is as if John is writing for that hankering in all of us to know what is going on at the very bottom of things, to know how things stand at the roots of reality. John shows us Jesus as the fundamental revelation of God's reality and ours—of God as the water of our lives, and of us as thirsty for God. Christ is indeed our cosmic Aquarius, sent by his Father to sate our thirst.

In the astrologers' picture, Aquarius is starry-bright, profiled against the blackness. But John also shows us Jesus as intimately at one with our need. When he describes the dying Lord on the cross, he tells us that he said, 'I am thirsty.' Well he might be, at such a moment, as the dying often are, and as we ourselves are likely to be one day. His being ready to be like that is a sign that he is ready to be with us in our own deepest thirsts, of body and of spirit. In this Mass, we thank him, as usual, both for his solidarity with us in need, and for his offer to refresh us in our mortal ways, and beyond them. For us, the Age of Aquarius will never be over.

*Newman: March, 1999*

LENT

# *Perishing?*
### 4th Sunday of Lent, Year B

I WAS BORN AND GREW UP IN THE CITY OF PERTH, on the western coast of Australia, about as physically remote from Washington DC as it is possible to get on the face of the Earth. When I was in high school, I used to go each day over a flight of stairs at the Perth Central railway station. And on the risers between some of the steps there were printed the words, 'God so loved the world that he sent his only-begotten Son so that anyone who believed in him should not perish.' I don't know that this did me any good: after all, I was young and self-congratulating and preoccupied with other matters; but at least I noticed it, and can report it to you about forty years later.

And well I might, not only because the words are the keynote of our Gospel passage today, but because they point to something at the heart of every human life. The word 'perish,' after all, is a formidable one: just as 'maim' sounds worse than 'injure', 'perish' sounds worse, even, than 'die'. Perishing is absolute—it is like vanishing, only more so: from perishing, there is no way back. Now Christian tradition has always held that, were it not for God's saving intervention, we should all perish. We may think of this in the sense that, failing God's continual creativity, we should perish into nothingness much faster than in the blink of an eyelid; and we may think of it in the sense that, failing God's continual mercy, we should be dragged into a hellish condition of moral nothingness, so that our human lives became, to adapt Thomas Hobbes' famous formulation, 'solitary, poor, nasty, brutish, and short'. But one way or the other, without God's immediate care, we would perish: and sometimes we come pretty close.

I have in my pocket at the moment a piece of paper on which there is a reference to this state of affairs, and probably you have, too. It is a dollar bill, with the words, 'In God we trust.' You can't get far with a dollar these days, and the piece of paper, six inches by two and a half inches, doesn't seem all that memorable. In the same way, the truth that God is our shield against perishing, morally and physically, is one which can be as neglected as the dollar in pocket or purse. Certainly, it can be deferred until some more urgent moment—if not the hour of our death, then at least the hour of emergency. After all, who of us wants to live like some saint in a seventeenth-century painting, staring-eyed, rapturous or agitated, with a skull on the table and an hour-glass at his elbow? Even if we can't say to that figure, 'Get a life!' we say it, in effect, to ourselves.

And yet, that inscription on the risers in Perth all those years ago was saying precisely that: 'Get a life!' Much of the time we live half-lives, or quarter-lives, harassed and harangued by external or internal voices which commend this thing, and scorn that thing, and demand that we dance to the tune of some other thing. What can happen in the midst of all this is that, day by day, my self, my soul, this little world loved by God, is frittered away into the un-world of the perished.

By contrast, as we are told in word and gesture hundreds of times in the New Testament, and more times still in the Old, what God yearns to give us, if we will only have it, is unstinted life. We cannot have this unless we concede, and confess, that there are places in our hearts which actively resist life, places where we cling to our greed, our anger, our self-preening, our self-hating: no good surgeon, after all, is going to try a transplant onto gangrenous tissue. Lent is a time when we pray to be honest about the gangrene, and also pray that we may be made sound again. We would be sentimentally foolish to make such a prayer unless we could put our trust in a God who knows how it goes with us. But such is our God; and the crucifix which is his insignia reminds us of what rejected life did to one human being, and also what accepted love can do for us all.

*Georgetown: March, 1997*

LENT

# The Expectation of Heaven
### 5th Sunday of Lent, Year C

AFTER YOU REACH A CERTAIN AGE, EVEN YOUR friends, let alone your enemies, can predict the sort of things you will complain about. Amongst other things, I complain that it is all too rare to hear a homily about Heaven: and since our second reading today is all about Heaven, I had better follow my own logic and try to say something about this precious topic.

Perhaps we hear so little about Heaven because for many people it is the equivalent of a fairyland, and most of us hear nothing about fairyland once we have moved on to more grown-up interests. Picturings of Heaven can be unsatisfactory, either because they represent somebody else's idea of a good time rather than our own—as, for instance, singing in large choirs organized by angels—or because they represent gratifications which are all too much our own, in that they seem selfish—as, for instance, being at an eternal, uninterrupted binge. Heaven is not much of a destination if it increases our solitude, or if it keeps us infantile.

St Paul tells us, and so does everybody else who thinks about the matter for a while, that we can't get any adequate picture of Heaven until we are there, which is not the evasion of the issue that it might seem. This present life of ours, after all, is one whose various phases or stages have their own distinctive character. Adolescence is a different experience from infancy, and being fifty is thought-provokingly different from being twenty. You have to be changed in order to have certain experiences, and you have to have had them in order to size them up. And yet there are things we can say about the condition of Heaven, and most of them have been said for us. I mention only two of them.

The first is that it will do justice, and more than justice, to our twin needs to be ourselves, and to be with the others. When our Lord was dying, and one of the men dying with him asked to be remembered when he came into his kingdom, Jesus replied, 'Today you will be with me in Paradise.' The conspicuous thing about the robber up there on his cross is the solitude of it all: you are left to yourself, and left by yourself, in your distress. That is a dreadful business, but such suffering has at least this to it, that it heightens your awareness of yourself as an absolute given: you know that any attempt to dissolve you away in explanation as just a ripple in society or an accident of biology is a pack of lies. There you are, aching not just in your body, but in your selfhood. And it was the robber's selfhood that was endorsed and forgiven and blessed by Jesus, and to that selfhood that Heaven was held out in prospect. Similarly, in our moments of greatest personal joy, when we sense ourselves to be, as we truly are, great instances and occasions of creativity, and in the strict sense unprecedented—at such moments we are in effect rumours of Heaven. We do not merely hear or pass on reverberations of the divine, we are those reverberations.

Each time our Lord attended with distinctive love to a person in distinctive need, he was endorsing and fortifying this unique work of his Father's hands. It might be the woman taken in adultery, or Lazarus caught in death's grip, or a man beset by demons, or even his own mother with her concern for a wedding feast liable to be overcast by disappointment. Whoever the person, and whatever the need, he did not respond just by doing jobs at large, but by touching, as it were, the live nerve of personality in the one immediately before him. This is to trace at once the presence of that person, and the presence of the Father who, from instant to instant, keeps just that person in being.

If the heavenly condition is one in which each of us will be more deeply endorsed for ever as the ones we are, it is also the state in which it will at last dawn on us how deeply inbound we are with one another. In word and deed, all through the gospels, our Lord is shown as bringing home to us this brute fact, this angelic fact, about us. To his disciples, wrangling and competing with one another, he says that he is the vine, and that they are the branches, and by implication that it is nonsense for any of them to suppose that he can grow, in the air, by himself. To anyone who will listen, he says that whoever gives a cup of water to anyone else, with Christ in mind, gives it to Christ. And of the Last Judgement, that occasion compared with which all earthly testings are as nothing, he says that the criterion of our becoming appropriate citizens of Heaven is our being open-hearted, and open-handed, towards the ragged and the ill and the jailed. Down at the point of deepest intimacy in each one of us, down deeper than chromosomal arrangement, is our daughtership or sonship towards God, and thus our sisterhood or brotherhood towards 'the others', since God is a God-for-others.

In the Eastern tradition of Christian liturgy and theology, this Mass, this process in which we are engaging at the moment, is seen as a foreshadowing of Heaven, or perhaps a limited but real flowing into time of eternity's condition, as the ocean, again and again, broaches a little the estuarial mouth of a river. Most of us have not been schooled to see things in that way: yet surely that tradition is right. For not only is it true that Jesus, the Lord who reigns in glory, will offer himself to us in our less-than-glorious condition at the moment of Communion: it is also true that each of us in this chapel shares it with others who, like ourselves, are called to an eternal communing. May we take them to heart as our Father takes us to heart: and may we give to them as he gives to us.

*Anglesea: April, 1995*

PASSION

# Christ the Palmer
## Palm Sunday

ALL OVER THE WORLD, AS IN THIS CHAPEL, THE green fronds with which we equip ourselves today are, most likely, not going to be palms, but palm-substitutes. But it is the only time in the Church's year that calls for attention to a piece of vegetation, so we may as well think about it.

Our only reason for thinking about it, though, is because it is an emblem of our Lord. It is, at least in the modern sense of the word, an icon of Christ—an icon of our life-giver, and heart-cherisher, and future-maker. So 'Palm Sunday' can provoke us once again to think about him, and about what he signifies to us. Let me say something about Jesus, the brother who saves us, on three counts. Each of them is precious. All of them have to do with what people have understood from palms.

The first is this: palms have been valued because they were fruitful. The fact is that palms may have been cultivated as least as long as wheat, or olives, or grapevines, because they have a thoroughly nourishing fruit, the date. Enormous treks across the Sahara and other deserts have been made mainly on the strength of dates—which is saying a good deal, since you could put almost the whole of Australia into the Sahara Desert. For millions of people whose names we will never know, the palm has been the very emblem of life, of sustenance. The palm has been, as it were, a palpable fountain: when you were failing, it kept you going.

The claim about Christ has been, from the first, that he is our nourisher: that he is like mothers' milk, is like dates in the desert and, more, like water in the desert. None of us has any business to be here today unless we think of this strange fellow in such terms. Christ is not precious because he is a sage, or because he is kindly, or because he is resolute. We can do with all the women and men we can get who are like that, of course: but this one is different. This one is the very embodied life of God himself, who is ready to have every human expression of that life snuffed out if that is what human beings insist upon—as they did—but who will be for us more than the best of mothers can ever be. Christ is the living palm, budding and fruiting for us beyond death.

The second thing about palms is that they became the standard badge or token for Christian pilgrims who were bound for Jerusalem. There were millions of them, over the span of Christianity so far. In the roughly one thousand years of what we call 'the middle ages', people risked life and limb to get to a very foreign place, because they found it made precious by our Lord's having walked its roads, and eaten under its trees, and died and risen from one of its hills.

But more importantly still, they knew that he, too, had been a pilgrim. They knew that, like his ancestors, he had gone up to Jerusalem to pray, and to be taught by God; and they knew that he had roved his little country in quest of others who might be hungry for God; and they knew that he had, at the end, gone the round of that pilgrimage for justice and love which we see represented around this chapel—the round we call 'the Stations of the Cross'. When, some years ago, Catholic thinkers and writers spoke of us all as a 'pilgrim people', and when this got picked up as the idiom of the teaching Church, they were all echoing the intuitive sense of millions of Christians whose names we will never know, in this world at least. Jesus was indeed someone who could not rest, and could not be himself, unless he was a God-hunter. The palms which became the insignia of yearning Christians from all over Christendom had to do with today's feast, when Jesus came into his intimately loved city, determined to find his Father's living presence there.

So the palms stand for nourishment, and they stand for

# Bread for the Journey

Christian quest. They also, traditionally, stand for victory. We have gone off this talk, to some extent, but there are still places where to be given (for instance) a 'Palm of Gold' is all the recognition you could want. A big palm-frond is like a banner, like a flag at the end of a big race: or, rather, they are like it—a living, gorgeous thing, green and sumptuous, embodying in effect both the journey of growth and the fruit to which it has given issue. In a week's time, on Easter Vigil night and then on Easter Sunday morning, all the talk will be of victory, or triumph. A late medieval poem from Scotland, by the poet William Dunbar, begins with the words, 'Done is the battle on the dragon black', and he is talking, accurately, about Christ's conquest of mortality, and viciousness, and demoralization, and futility. Dunbar, on behalf of us all, is boasting about Christ's triumph: Dunbar is, as we call priests at Mass, our celebrant.

Dunbar is right. And we are all right, every one of us, to come like pilgrims up the aisle, and to receive the bread and the wine, the milk and the dates, of Christ's living presence. Our challenge, not just through the week ahead, but through the long week of our lives, is to continue to live by the faith and hope that Jesus Christ, mortal and divine, is the vindicator of life, whatever the dragon may say or do. I wish you well in this, my brothers and sisters: but far more importantly, so does He.

*Newman: March, 1999*

GOOD
FRIDAY

# *Making the Crooked Straight*
**Good Friday**

THE GOSPEL ACCOUNT OF OUR LORD'S PASSION, to which we have just listened, is a story of many things that are out of true, many things that are 'askew'. There are more emphatic things to be said about it—that it is a tale of betrayal, and judicial murder; that it is full of disappointment, and of disarray; worst of all, perhaps, that it is full of pain, and pain at many levels. But the familiar story speaks for itself, and our ritual re-enacts its meaning, so I want to make only one simple point about it. Which is this.

As we all know, in this century, a twisted version of the cross became dreadfully familiar to many millions of people throughout the world—that version which we call the swastika. Centuries ago that sign was harmless enough, and even benign: but there was nothing benign about its modern significance. What it came to stand for, at least to the helpless who were in its shadow, was stultification, termination, and vileness. As part of the work of the devil, it announced that there was no hope for most of humanity, and that all our deeds and works were worthless, and that the best that could be hoped for was death.

Dreadful things still happen in our world today, some of them at the hands of just such people as were once proud to wear the swastika. And these things are not only publicly violent and vicious: most of them, in fact, go on un-noticed except by those who are their per-

43

petrators and their victims. But what we put our faith in today—that, even, we celebrate—is the fact that Jesus, the cruciform man upon his cross, straightens out the diabolical crookedness of the swastika, and leaves us, all of us, with the possibility of going the paths of love and arriving at love's vindicating destination. The agonized Jesus, matching the agony with love, points our way home.

We know this, as Christians have always known it. It is because this is so that, when we trace the figure of the cross on our bodies, we say that we are 'blessing' ourselves; and when, as Christians, we seek blessings—at the end of the sacrament of reconciliation, or at the end of the Eucharist, or at some private moment—we expect the tracery of the cross then, too. So as we contemplate the figure of the crucified Lord this afternoon, we do so, always and only, to take heart.

But as we do so, we should remember this: the abolishing of the swastika's crookedness, the devil's crookedness, does not leave us with a single pole, a line and nothing else. All responsible human being, all ripening love, brings us time and again to choices, to cross-roads. Every human figure who is named or noticed in the Passion narrative is someone charged with choice. And so it is with us. We need our seasons of passivity: even our hearts need to sleep sometimes, whether they are wounded or they are whole. But life is choice; love is choice; Christianity is choice. In a little while we will pray together for that world which is much dearer to God than it can ever be to us—will pray that good and fruitful choices be made. Let us pray for one another, and for ourselves, that we may be braved to choose in the fashion of Christ, who blesses our crossroads.

*Newman: April, 1999*

RESURRECTION

# *Magnolias*
**Easter Day**

SOME OF YOU WILL HAVE SEEN ONE OR another of David Attenborough's natural history or wild life programs on television, and you may also have read the books written in connection with these. One of those books is called *The Private Life of Plants*—an accurate, if rather cute title, since it often has to do with many features of plant life which take place invisibly or secretly. And in that book Attenborough reports that, in 1982, when an ancient settlement in Japan was being excavated, the scientists dug up a two-thousand-year-old harvest pit which contained at the bottom some blackened, dead, grains of rice. In their midst was one seed which was different. They took it out, and planted and watered it, and it sprang to life. It was a magnolia.

It is not hard to guess why I mention this today. Easter Day, in this, its original hemisphere, falls at a time of year when one expects to see defiant outbursts of new life—as, for instance, in the crocuses which get themselves up in the beds outside this chapel, and over so much of this country, and in so many other countries. We like the look of them not only because they are often handsome, but because of their vitality: the frost and snow, the wind-chill and the frigid earth have not had the last word about them; their flowering is a flourishing, and they have the flair of life itself.

You would not bet on this if you saw a northern winter for the

45

first time, and knew no better. And certainly, you would not bet on the resurgence of the magnolia from its one seed, down among the dead. And yet so it was. If we were in the business of re-inventing or re-naming symbols, we might call it the Magnolia of Christ, because it stands so vividly for an indispensable truth about him—that he is *the* resurrected mortal, in the power of whose rising all of us are also being raised.

Some things about Christ's person and fortunes are unknown, or unimportant, or both. His mother must have known and cared how he looked, but none of us knows, and there is not much use our caring about it. If he had a favourite game, or food, or colour, or tune, or joke, we know nothing about it; if he had a favourite rabbinical teacher, or political thinker, or sharer of insights, we know nothing about that either. The truly indispensable thing about him, which got the Christian fuss started and has kept it going to the point where you and I are here together today, is that he was truly raised from a true death, and that this happened not simply because God our Father took special pity on one individual, but because it would be intolerable that a human being who had, because also divine, kept total faith with the God of life, should be left in the cold grip of death. And not only intolerable: impossible.

My brothers and sisters, there are countless paintings of the rising or risen Christ, some of which are a waste of good canvas, and some of which are permanent parts of the glory of humanity. But good or bad, they are all misleading unless they manage to signal the fact that the rising Lord carries us with him as he goes. That magnolia-seed in Japan, about two thousand years old, took root, and eleven years later produced its first flower bud; the following year, there were over thirty flowers on the tree. The inrush, or uprush, of life from the seed took its branching way into new buds, new births. And this is the way it was, and is, with the rising of the Lord. He spoke, you remember, of himself as vine and of us as branches: he might, had he been born in Japan, have spoken of magnolias and their branching.

Since all this is so, how are we to respond? In two ways, surely. The first is in the fashion of people who have been given the best of news—that all that is physically and morally and spiritually most deathly has been beaten decisively: we are to rejoice. So we do, ritually, here, with the lights and the music and the food and drink: and so we do, though often in more muted fashion, whenever this re-enacting of the resurrection of the mortal Lord into immortality is announced. And the other response, which requires sobriety, and tenacity, and sometimes the faith of those who feel winter's profound chilling, is in the living out of the truth that we are indeed all of one stock with the vine, of one stock with the magnolia. True, anyone you see today or for the rest of your life will be at best a frail member of that one living body: but then so are you—and look what has happened on your behalf.

*Georgetown: March, 1997*

EASTER

# *Twinned with Thomas*

## 2nd Sunday of Easter, Year A

IN THE GOSPEL PASSAGE WE HAVE JUST HEARD, there is a detail which has always intrigued me. Thomas, who is an absentee when Christ appears to the other disciples, and who is a dissident when he returns, is also someone of whom we are told that his name means 'twin'. Perhaps he did indeed have a twin brother or twin sister, and if he did, then that man or woman may, as twins often are, have been much the sort of person he was. If so, they would have a good dose of scepticism about them. Like Thomas, they would believe that it is only fools who rush in where the wise fear to tread: and, like Thomas, they would be pretty reserved about the clamouring enthusiasm of other people. They would be inclined to say, as often as not, 'count me out'.

I don't know whether Thomas actually had a twin: perhaps his name was a nickname; perhaps it was something like those surnames of many people of our own day, which allude to someone in our family tree rather than ourselves—not all people called 'Baker' are bakers, and not all people called 'Falconer' go about the world with large predatory birds perched on their wrists. But what I would suggest is that many Australians, and perhaps many of us, are in effect the twins of Thomas. And this can be good news, or it can be bad news.

It is good news in so far as it is healthy to be sceptical of the drift and clamour of public opinion in the conduct of our lives. Public opinion can say, or imply, that you are only as good as you look, or that you are worth only what you own, or that you count only as much as your career does. Public opinion, come to that, can clamour that Aborigines do not count, or that Jews do not, or that ethnic Albanians do not. All of these claims of public opinion are lies, and some of them are lethal lies. St Thomas the Sceptic is a good person to pray to, a good person to hope to be twinned with, when such lies are abroad, and when they are powerful.

But the bad news about being twinned with Thomas only in his mode, and his moments, of rejection, is that the human agenda, and the Christian agenda, cannot be lived through in that way. We were created for flourishing, the whole lot of us: were conceived and born for flourishing. We are in this Chapel right now to thank God that he flourishes among us, and that he gives us the Holy Spirit of flourishing from one instant to the next. Sometimes we can gather this truth in solitude—it can come to us in the instant of our turning a book's page, or in the milli-second of our glance at a tree, at any season of the year. But very often we will need the witness of others—will need the voices of other men and women, young and old, all of them frail like ourselves, but all of them capable, too, of bearing us the best of news: the news that our lives are not accidental or incidental, that our personalities are not just the upshot of blind genetic forces, that our days and years are not simply a tick of the sun's clock or the earth's clock, but that all of this is something given its warrant, and its goal, by a Christ wounded to death by the world's troubled ways, but now sustained immortally as our cherishing brother.

Many years ago, I wrote a poem prompted by this Gospel passage. In the poem, I imagine people who are indeed twinned with the sceptical Thomas, the misgiving Thomas, pleading—even demanding—that the risen Christ show his wounds, so that they may be sure that it is no hocus-pocus that is being worked on them. The poem was written to be set to music, and the composer, Fr Christopher Willcock, gave it a grandeur of which I had not thought, but which was in fact true to the spirit of this Gospel passage. May none of us neglect the wounds of our world: but may all of us be blessed with a faith in that wounded Christ made immortal in his love.

*Newman: April, 1999*

EASTER

# *At the End of the Day*
### 3rd Sunday of Easter, Year A

SOME OF YOU MAY REMEMBER A POEM WHICH WE have looked at together, a poem called 'C Minor'. It is by the American poet Richard Wilbur, and it begins with his saying to his wife that she was right to turn off the radio when, at breakfast time, it began to broadcast Beethoven's Fifth Symphony: it seemed too much for the occasion. Then Wilbur imagines what the day, a typical day, may bring for the two of them—the bright or dark things, the ins and outs; and he suggests that they have music at the end of the day when there will be, he says, 'something to organize'.

All days, and all years, bring us 'something to organize'. Work or relaxation, problems and pleasures, the rise and fall of relationships, opportunities and accomplishments and disappointments, sweet apples and sour ones—'Such Is Life', as Joseph Furphy called the most famous Australian novel, and as Ned Kelly said just before he died. As we get older— not old, just older—we value being able to find some meaning or pattern in the torrent of events, big and small. Macbeth thought that life was a tale told by an idiot, signifying nothing: but Macbeth was a hagridden murderer, and most of us hold to the hopes which he had let slip from his grasp. 'At the end of the day', as people often say nowadays, 'at the end of the day' we want things to be organized out of idiocy, and into meaning and value.

In today's Gospel, the decisive moment comes at the end of the day. We have the story of two dejected ex-followers of Jesus who are tramping off to a village about as far from Jerusalem as from here to Balwyn or to Brighton. They have been raking over recent events with a mysterious stranger, who has been shedding light on those events for them. When they are nearly at their destination, it looks as if they are going to lose touch with him, and they say, 'Look, stay with us: it's pretty well the end of the day.' They need more light in their lives, just when the light of the day is waning. They have plenty of chaotic experience, and they are not travelling well with it. They have 'something to organize': what they need is an orchestrating presence.

Notice what our Lord does *not* do. He does not make light of what has happened to them—the dismaying and disgusting events of the last few days, and the part they may have played in those events. And he gives full weight to the feeling of helplessness, of being pawns in the hands of indifferent or malevolent powers, which we can all have, and some of us have often. He faces hard into their past, as, very recently, beaten bloody, he had faced hard into his present. It is only when that is done, and through its being done, that he names providence, implies mercy, and eventually sits down and eats with them.

Shared eating stands for shared need, and for shared love. It is because we are frail, even the most broad-shouldered of us, that we eat, and because we fear loneliness that we do not want to eat alone. And it is because we can love and be loved that we choose to eat together, sharing space and food and time as a way of sharing ourselves. Christ, lately come from the cross, was an authority on frailty and loneliness: but the same Christ, freshly drawn into unkillable life, was also an authority on the love that abolishes loneliness. Walking with his recovering disciples, and then eating with them, he was indeed helping them to 'organize' their lives, as Beethoven, astoundingly, organized the sounds of our lives.

There are, surely, lessons for all of us to learn from this remarkable story. They are lessons about looking for insight even in the midst of distress; and about being ready to give up our griefs when that becomes possible—a harder thing, sometimes, than it sounds; and about handing on to others whatever of life's good news has come our way, instead of basking in it in a self-centred way. The men on the way to—it might have been Brighton, and it might have been Balwyn—stand for all of us. But let me suggest that instead of being over-anxious to extract a lesson from this Gospel passage, we take a little time to do with it what we would do with the Fifth Symphony: to *hear* it, that is, and more than once, patiently and gratefully. If we do that, it will organize more than a day.

*Newman: April, 1993*

EASTER

# Christ as Misfit, as Venturer, as Way

5th Sunday of Easter, Year A

I WANT TO SPEAK TO YOU TODAY ABOUT OUR Lord under three aspects; and I want to do this because, in the gospels, and in today's Gospel, he does keep showing himself to us in different lights. When you think about it, this is one of the things which can make him credible to us. Any human being whom we can take seriously is ready to be seen in a variety of ways or lights. Most of the figures who insist on being seen in only one stereotyped fashion are either fakes, buffoons, or tyrants. There they are, on the posters or in the photographs, or even (God help them) in public, looking the same—as if they were eternal, as if they were divine. And if we do not make the mistake of worshipping them, we realize that their pretensions are rubbish. Anyone who is reducible to his or her single image is a mere idol—which means, a phoney.

By contrast, our Lord is ready to be caught in many guises, and at many moments. One of them is that of the *misfit*. In the gospels, there is not a single example, I think, in which he is entirely and naturally at ease, socially. It is as if there is always something 'left over' about him, almost in the mathematical sense. He is a puzzler, a provoker, a summoner. He is the sort of person who, if you are organizing a party or some other sociable occasion, you would know that you had to invite because he was so special, but about whom you would be a bit worried because he might be a bit of a problem at the

53

event—not by getting drunk or by being quarrelsome or boringly emphatic, but by making other people feel, just by his quality, that something significant still called for attention. Our Lord was the joker in the pack, the square peg in society's round hole. He was word from somewhere else—word for us, but still word from somewhere else.

A second image I have for Christ is that of the *venturer*. We hear a lot these days, in some circles, about 'venture capital'—money on the loose, looking to see where it can reproduce itself. I know nothing about those financial ways: but what I do know is that, when people are at the peak of their personal vitality, they are ready to venture their time and energy and ingenuity in growing beyond where they are, currently. This is the sort of figure our Lord cuts in the gospels. He is prone to say things like, 'You have heard that you should love those who love you: all right, I am telling you to love those who hate you.' This is very unsatisfactory to most of us, much of the time. For it really is hard enough to love those who love us, as the years unfold; we can get bored with them, and we can disagree with them, and we can simply get exhausted and not be on for loving anybody in particular, not even ourselves. And to be told, still, to love our enemies! 'Give us a break!', we may feel. But he will not give us a break. He wants us to make our run for the border of love, and beyond. He wants us to be venturers. All of us—you, unfortunately; and me, even more unfortunately.

And thirdly, my dears, our Lord offers himself as *'the way'*—the way to fulness of life, the way to the wellsprings of creation, the way to the Father who, having fathered us, must now continue to cherish us for eternity. Please God, we have all had some sense of how Jesus the Chosen One, Jesus the limping brother, can be the Way for all of us; that is why we are here—to be bonded once again with his words, with his fleshed-out presence, with his living siblings. We grasp intuitively, even if we cannot put words to it— and why should we want to?—that he's the Way. But I have a final word to you today which adds something to that, and it is this.

Christ the Misfit endorses our own lack of perfect 'fit' in the world: because none of us fits in perfectly, and we were never meant to, no matter what anyone else says. Christ the Venturer endorses our own hankering to grow, in spirit, in radical humanity, beyond conventionally set agendas: and he prompts us to try, again and again, to love more ambitiously than we have bargained for, so far. And Christ the Way can, and does, make each of us *someone else's* way to flourish, not only here and now, but through the long Spring of eternity.

There is a Spanish proverb that says, 'God writes straight with crooked lines.' All of us, to some degree, are crooked: but God can make us the straightest way to him for somebody else. And perhaps, for most of us, that will be the best thing we can do or be in this life—to be the living way to God's home and ours, for another of his daughters, or his sons. Here, at this Mass, let us eat and drink with some of those others on their personal journeys. And let us take heart, once more, for our own.

*Newman: May, 1999*

EASTER

## The Mind's Guests
### 6th Sunday of Easter, Year C

THERE IS ONE PARTY OF PHILOSOPHERS WHICH SAYS that we are born with some of our ideas ready-made, wired-in as it were: and there is another which says that we aren't—that it is we ourselves who do all the work from scratch. At the moment it doesn't matter which of these parties is right. What matters is the kind of welcome that we give to ideas, and how we go about cherishing some and ejecting others. Not any and all ideas, of course. It doesn't really matter whether I put my left shoe on first in the morning or my right shoe, so it's harmless enough if I have fixed ideas about the matter. And it doesn't really matter if I can't name correctly all the countries of Africa, and if I confidently suppose that one of them is called, say, 'Branga'. You might as well leave me alone in my ignorance, and I might as well leave myself alone about these matters too.

What do matter, though, are the major ideas and convictions to which I give a home in my mind. They will be the things which determine all sorts of decisions and policies without my being very aware of it. The movers and shakers of the world, for many hundreds of years, have been very clear about this. The whole prodigious advertising and propaganda enterprise which affects each of us every day works on that principle. The wars fought, and still being fought, in so many parts of the world, are fuelled not mainly by the oil in the tanks and the cartridges in the gunbelts, but by the ideas which have been

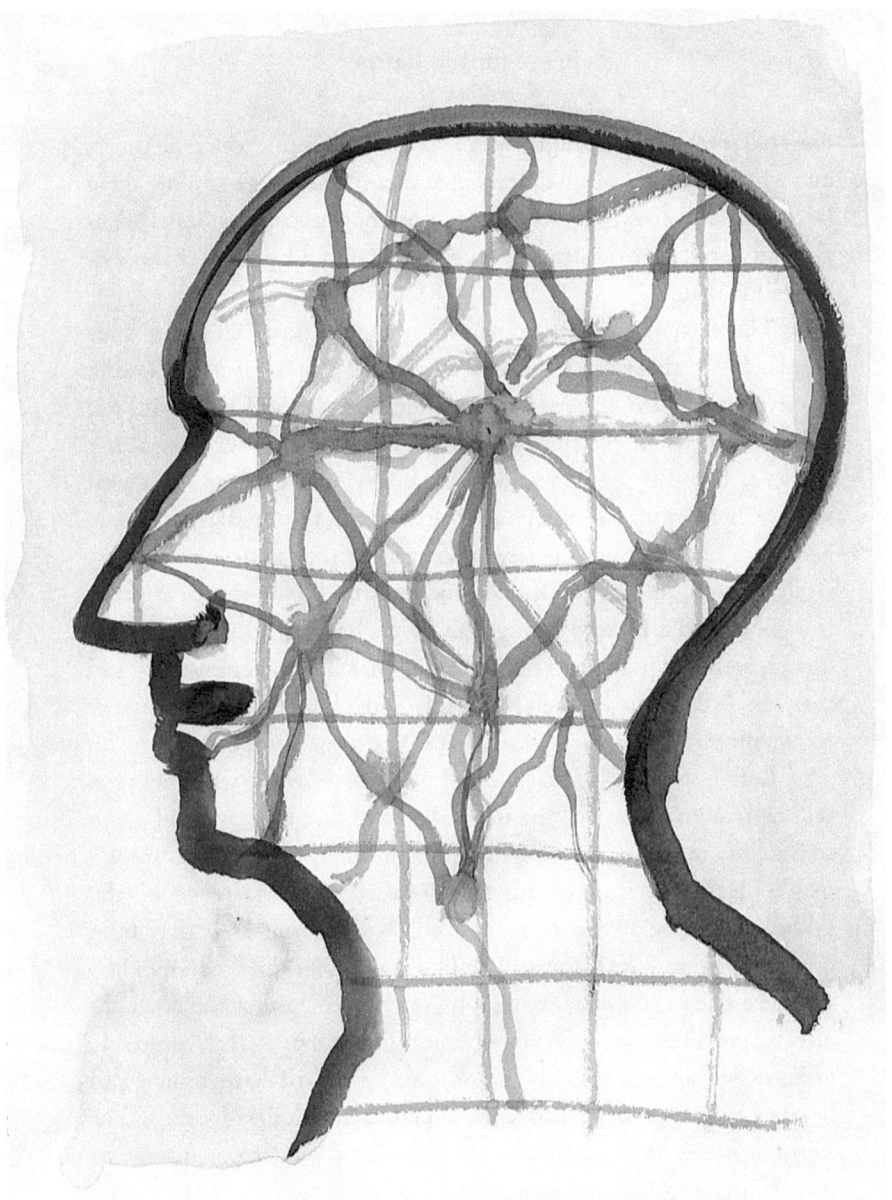

'The wars fought, and still being fought, in so many parts of the world, are fuelled not mainly by the oil in the tanks and the cartridges in the gunbelts, but by the ideas which have been inserted into people's minds, which have been given welcome there, and which have as a result determined their decisions.'

inserted into people's minds, which have been given a welcome there, and which have as a result determined their decisions. To follow them becomes, as we say, 'second nature'. Many of those particular ideas are bad news, and the trail of bodies left behind by them is the evidence for that.

There is, though, a whole array of good-news ideas. In their secular form, these are represented by much of what is negotiated in a university, and in other forms of education. If the Church did not believe this, we might all be at Mass at the moment, but it wouldn't be here, because there wouldn't be a Newman College. In a real sense, Christianity has often been the cradle of universities, precisely because Christians have believed, correctly, that ideas can be massively meaningful, massively good and fruitful. So the secular context is a good, and a blessed, thing. But as we listened to the Gospel, a complementary point was being made: that it is no one less sacred than the Father, the Son, and the Holy Spirit who bids for admission to our minds, and who claims rights in our consciousness.

Our Lord says, in that Gospel passage, 'Anyone who loves me will be true to my word, and my Father will love him; we will come to him and make our home with him'; and then he promises to send us the Holy Spirit, who might be called the Heartener of the Disheartened, to live with us as well. Now it isn't as if they have nowhere else to go: that would be like saying that the ecosystem had nowhere else to go unless we let it in, or that the cosmos had nowhere else to go unless we gave it a home. The point is that, precisely because we are the God-begotten ones, we will have minds and hearts which are askew, deformed and mutilated, unless we do accept into the home of our consciousness the God who, from instant to instant, gives us that consciousness.

You don't need to be a theologian to do this, or a person of great intellectual brilliance, or even particularly pious. Most Christians have not been any of these things, and were never meant to be. What you need to do is, in the first place, to take seriously the words of the Gospel—reading them again today, from St John's fourteenth Chapter, couldn't hurt any of us—and in the second place, to keep your eyes and ears open to see where, within the next twenty-four hours, you have an opportunity to do what God does best, in fact all that he does—namely, to love.

If you do make this your policy, you might remember where God started in loving you. It wasn't in that you were brilliant, beautiful, and the best thing since sliced bread, but that you were someone in *need*. If you don't, one way or another, in the next twenty-four hours, identify someone in need of your loving contribution, the chances are that you are not listening as hard as you might be to the God who makes a home in you, every day. That would be a pity. And you are the only one in the whole wide world who can change it.

*Newman: May, 1995*

## ASCENSION

# *Keep in Touch*
## Ascension Day, Year A

THIS IS THE FEAST OF THE ASCENSION OF OUR LORD into Heaven, so I shall say a few words, briefly, about Garrison Keillor. Garrison Keillor will be known to some as the man who, for a number of years, mounted a weekly radio program in America, a program often replayed in Australia. In it, he spoke about the sayings and doings of a fictitious township in Minnesota, called Lake Wobegon. Like millions of other people, I have heard a lot of these programs, and although I know that they are about a fiction I also know that they are telling many truths. So I am well-disposed towards Garrison Keillor.

A few years ago, when I was doing some teaching in Washington DC, I found that Keillor had another program on the radio. This was a daily one, and it was very short—about five minutes long. It was called 'The Writers' Almanac', and it had a few details about various writers, ancient and modern, and often a poem being read. But it always ended with a wish, or a directive, from Keillor, which went, 'Be well, do good work, and keep in touch.' I liked this saying very much, and I still do—partly because it fits so well with today's feast.

Our Lord, in the Gospel passage we have heard, leaves his followers with a triple charge. Firstly, he reiterates his own authority as God's own Son, and he authorizes those who believe in him to bond others with themselves in a belief in him. He tells them—he tells us, which is the reason we are listening to his word today—he tells them, and us, to keep in touch with him, and with one another, and with those among whom we move. This sounds fine as a formula, but since we are all adults we know that it is also exacting. It is exacting because most of us feel so clumsy when we pray, and therefore wonder whether it is worthwhile; and it is exacting because busyness, or worry, or boredom, or scepticism, can slow up our readiness to go on opening our hearts and minds to our fellow Christians; and it is exacting because plenty of Australians want no part not only of the Catholic Church, or of Christianity, but of anything religious or sacred at all. *And still*, in the Australia of mid-1999, the Lord of Heaven and Earth, the wounded and radiant Jesus, presses us to try once more to 'keep in touch' with God, and with our fellow Christians, and with our fellow citizens and compatriots.

So much for keeping in touch. There is also the matter of doing good work. In our Gospel passage, the Lord gives his followers tasks. He tells them that they are to win the various countries and cultures to allegiance to him, and that they are to steep them in an awareness of God's creative and saving presence, and that they are to offer just such illumination as Christ brought to his first followers. Well, this is good work: this is worth the venture: worth our intelligence, and our passion, and our being re-made in whatever ways are necessary so that we can play our part. When you think about it, those great culture-heroes of Christianity whom we call saints—the old ones and the new ones—are never remembered, or cherished, simply because they can be certified as having had appropriately pious attitudes. They are remembered because they got on with doing something about the divine and human vision which had been offered to them, as it is offered to us. Sometimes what they did took the form of creatively accepted suffering— which is hard enough work, God knows—and sometimes it took the form of almost ceaseless exertion. But the animating element in it all, like the filament in a lightbulb, was their consciousness that Christ had worked on our behalf—teaching, healing, and (perhaps hardest of all) listening and listening—to bring humanity, once and for all, into God's own milieu. That was good work: and it still is.

## Bread for the Journey

Garrison Keillor's first tag of all was, 'Be well.' I used to listen to his short programs while I was shaving in the morning, and at such a moment I did not feel at my most commanding; it was after the helplessness of sleep, and before the coffee kicked in. So to 'be well' sounded, partly, like just another thing to cope with, and certainly not something entirely at my command. But the slogan can still heighten our alertness to the fact that God himself is our resource, and our recourse: that God is our health. Which means that health, at least health of spirit, is there to be had: and that to be with God is a healthy way to be.

This is not a glib saying. Our Lord, who called himself the doctor or healer, and who healed bodies, minds and hearts, was utterly realistic about the common run of human affairs—if you want to know about sickness, ask a doctor or a nurse. And, at the end of his short life's exertions for us all, he was not, to put it mildly, a well man. But at the very end, in the gospel account, he surrendered his mortal being to his immortal Father, the source and vindication of his life, as the Father is the source and vindication of our lives. Our Lord, a teacher to the last, was showing us where health's wellsprings lie: he was offering himself to be touched back to unkillable life, and, in love's embrace, offering us as well for that same touch. He was, himself, for all his drastic need, being well. In doing this for no other reason than our need, he was doing good work— the best in fact. And, supremely, he was keeping in touch with the Father, and with that Spirit who is Love personified for Father and Son and our own needy selves.

I don't know how Garrison Keillor is these days: we might all spare him a prayer, since I hope that his words have been doing us some good. What I do know is that the Lord of health and good heart, the Lord of worthwhile tasks carried through to the end, the Lord of unbroken solidarity with divinity and the children of divinity—that Lord goes on towering before us today. Whatever else the Feast of the Ascension means, it means that Christ is walking tall still, and walking for us.

*Newman: May, 1999*

PENTECOST

# *Crowd and Community*
## Pentecost Sunday, Year C

IF YOU POKE AROUND IN THE CATALOGUE OF THE Baillieu Library at Melbourne University, you will find a number of books with the word 'crowd' in their titles. There is *The Crowd in History*, and *The Crowd in the French Revolution*, and *The Crowd and the Mob*. This makes sense, because when you think about it an enormous amount of history has to do with crowd-behaviour, in war and in peace. This is just as true of our own time, in which the world as a whole is much more crowded than ever before.

'Mob' is a word for an unpleasant thing—an unthinking, possibly violent crush together of human beings prone to behave in a sub-human way: it's appropriate that one nickname for organized crime is 'The Mob'. But even 'crowd' sounds fairly uncomplimentary: it suggests a kind of lowest common denominator amongst the people who make it up. By contrast, another word, 'community', when it is being used with some care, implies a sharing of strengths, and even a mutual fostering of individuality, in that the communing persons become more themselves, not less, by their cooperating as they do.

The reason I am saying these things is that one way of thinking of Pentecost is to see it as the conversion of a crowd into a community. In our first reading today, we heard of a swarm of people from an array of nationalities clustered together in Jerusalem—a crowd there for a worthy purpose, but still a crowd. Then there is an intervention by the Holy Spirit, and as a result of this, without the

'... when you think about it
an enormous amount of history
has to do with crowd-behaviour,
in war and peace. This is just as true
of our own time, in which the world
as a whole is much more crowded
than ever before.'

Parthians and the Romans and the Egyptians and the rest of them losing touch with their own languages and all that languages can stand for, they are made one in their hearing the challenging and heartening Word of God.

Conventionally, that moment is regarded as the birthday of the Church, so that people are called together (as we are right now) not only because of human initiatives and for pragmatic purposes, but through God's initiative and for his purposes, though these of course are always deployed through human occasions, since that is what the Incarnation means. But as with our own individual births, there is an awful lot of growing and changing required of the new-born Christian community.

Fear, and greed, and competitiveness, and smouldering angers—the sorts of things that flourish in mobs—are always a temptation to communing Christians, just as they can be in any individual woman or man. And more than that, the outward-reaching generosity, the creativity of spirit, which should be the hallmark of authentic Christianity, can dwindle away into a 'let's get the wagons into a circle and gloom together inside them', in the face of human intractability. There are hundreds of thousands of landmines, those evil things, throughout the world, maiming and killing individuals like you and me every day. But there are also what might be called landmines in our hearts too, instruments and forces which attack all that is best and most generous in us.

Which is why the Sequence we also heard is as pertinent as ever today. We prayed there, in a poetical way, for moral bravery, for fertility of spirit, for a humaneness which will be at once God's gift and a principle of union amongst us. We prayed with one eye on our present world's disconcerting needs, and with another on that greater world for which we are all bound. The more someone does attempt to engage with those present needs, the more they will be aware that this calls for more resources than we can muster of ourselves: it takes divine power to make for human goodness. So let us pray together today, we who are not a mob, we who are more than a crowd, to be receptive to the power the Spirit is so eager to share with us. We won't see the Easter Candle on display again this year: but there is a candle of hope and prayer to be carried in our hearts.

*Newman: June, 1995*

TRINITY

# *Threefold Love*
**Trinity Sunday, Year A**

SOME PEOPLE, WHEN THEY ARE WRITING, NEED absolute silence: the great novelist Marcel Proust wrote in a cork-lined room, and good luck to him. Others, including probably some here present, like to have music running in the background. Occasionally I am like that, and what I usually have going, God help me, is that golden oldie, Don McLean singing 'American Pie'. And there is in that, as you all recall, a moment when the wistful singer says that 'the three men I admire most/ the Father, Son and Holy Ghost/ they caught the last train for the coast/ the day the music died.'

This is not high theology, but it is certainly relevant to our feast today. The revelation that the one God is three-fold in power, three-fold in love, is not something given to humanity just so that we could note it as fact—an exceedingly remote fact like the greatest and most distant of all those billions of stars the science-writers tell us about. We are shown it, we are told it, in the sort of context provided by our passage from St John's Gospel today, where our Lord says, outright, 'God so loved the world that he gave his only Son, that whoever believes in him may not die but may have eternal life. God did not send the Son into the world to condemn the world, but so that the world might be saved through him.'

This means that the loved world is like a loved child—far from flawless, but embraced, nourished, taught, led and healed. It means that however bad things do get here, however violent or malevolent or cynical or steeped in selfishness individuals or societies may become, it is not open to God to give up on the world: the unbreakable cables of his love hold him to us. It means that, do what we may with ruinous weapons in our hands or with the ruinous weapons in our hearts, when the smoke clears and while the stench rises, God will still be there, the One who cannot get away.

If we are honest, we must say that it does not always look like this: often, it does not look like this at all. We do not have to sup together on the grossest of horrors, the mindless or calculated butcheries north and south and east and west in the world. Many of us, instead, can think of personal lesions, which have left parts of us scarified for the rest of our lives: personal desertions or betrayals, riptides in our health, dead-ends to our prospects which have come up in the night, as the Berlin Wall was built overnight to stifle the elementary human freedoms of half a people. Don McLean's plaint that the divine custodians of love have moved out on us, have left us for dead, sounds pretty much like the last word.

Of course, if we did, through and through, believe that it was the last word, none of us would be here today: we would be elsewhere, either having as good a time as possible, or making the best of a bad job, which sounds like much the same sort of thing. We are here, I hope, not because somebody has bullied us into thinking that if we were not here things would get even worse, but because the steady, modest, tender voices of Father, Son and Holy Ghost have gone on being heard in our hearts, to say that they do indeed love us, come what may, and that we would do well to stand and sit and kneel in company with others who have heard the voicing of that love. We are here because the divine ones are here: and they, astoundingly, are here because we are here.

That may be common ground among us, and I hope that it is. But when we begin any Eucharist, any Mass, and invoke the Blessed Three, we also embark once more on the old Christian journey, in which we attempt, in spite of our memories and our fears, to re-learn to love the world. The levels, the pitches, at which this can be done are countless. You may do nothing more important in your whole life than to give a cup of water to some thirsty unknown passer-by: the Samaritan woman at an old well did that, and everything changed for her, and for many others. You may battle, in the midst of angers and disappointments, to name a good way for human beings to go in life's forest: Dante did that in his epic poem of ultimate happiness, though he wrote it all in exile, and if he had gone back to his native city he would have been burned alive. You may take the intricate trails of ordinary human endeavour, things which often look like mazes, with the time, as it does for all of us after a while, running out at a rate we wouldn't have believed possible: if you do, that aligns you with every saint, named or anonymous, who has ever lived.

In any of these circumstances, the summons comes, many times, not to deny love: not to decline to accept it, not to decline to give it. There is no great skill involved in all this. Giving or receiving love is not like doing astrophysics, or besting Yehudi Menuhin with a violin, or making some competitor at the Olympic Games look silly: a cup of cold water can do it, provided the man and the woman can step beyond ancient hatreds, ancient fears.

The great, but fierce, Christian thinker Blaise Pascal wrote in his notebook that 'the self can always be hated'. We can do it to ourselves, we can do it to other selves, and we can certainly do it to God; personally, I think that it is mainly to God that we do it—God is the one where all the grudges come home in the end. What today's feast of the Blessed Three says to us is that this is all a blunder, a mistake about how things truly are. If we do insist on declining love, in the end nobody, not even God, can stop us: you can ram a lot of things down somebody's throat, but you can't ram love down. But to decline love remains a mistake, first, last, and always. As we eat Love's meal together today, let us pray for one another that we may continue to come to our senses. After all, there is so much to receive, and there is so much to give.

*Newman: June, 1996*

BODY OF
CHRIST

# *The Embodiment of God*

**Corpus Christi, Year A**

How do you feel about bears? Black bears, I mean, and brown bears, and polar bears, and all the rest of them? There is a fair bit of good-will towards them around—think of Pooh Bear, and Paddington Bear, and Teddy Bear. Some cultures have thought of bears as sacred: up in the sky there are figures known as the Greater Bear and the Lesser Bear, and one of the greatest theologians of the twentieth century, Hans Urs von Balthasar, appears to have been named after a bear.

Oddly enough, I am asking about bears because this is the feast of the Body and Blood of Christ. What I have in mind is a poem by the American Delmore Schwartz, a poem about the body, which begins 'The heavy bear who goes with me …' As poets will, he is tilting in from a new angle on something familiar. No doubt it is true that the heavier the person, the heavier the bear; but light or heavy, our bodies are around all the time, 'going' with us: and light or heavy, we are likely to be in two minds about them.

When things go well, we are all for bodies. There they are, alert in their five senses, moving about when asked, fitting into the world's processes, able to fuel themselves at need, capable of reproducing themselves, the sources and instruments and occasions of much happiness. When things go badly, we look at them darkly. If they are in pain, they clamour at us; if we are downcast, it is a tedious thing to have to drag them around; and they do, certainly, have a way

'How do you feel about bears?
Black bears, I mean, and brown bears,
and polar bears, and all the rest of them?
There is a fair bit of good-will towards
them around—think of Pooh Bear, and
Paddington Bear, and Teddy Bear.'

of getting out of hand, so that our mirrors tell us sad stories, and our consciences turn in bad reports on them.

But for better or for worse, for richer or for poorer, in sickness or in health, where would we be without them? The curious thing is that they give us both our privacy and our publicness, our internal life and our shared lives. You can use your face to mask your feelings or to show them: you can use any amount of body-language to welcome people or to rebuff them. The body, in other words, is complex—not only as an organism with all its framework and juices and processes, but as a displayer and performer of meanings. If bodies are not the only show in town, there is certainly no show without them.

We celebrate today the embodied condition of Christ our Lord. This has what might be called three phases. There is the *Christmas* embodiment—the small, still-wet body, come among us for a human life's duration, the body which is to end, wet once more, this time with sweat and blood, on a cross. There is the *liturgical* or *ceremonial* embodiment, in which we share at this moment, where our Lord comes home to us once more via our own senses and the meanings we find through them—in the transformed bread and wine, which would have no meaning except as offered for our eating; in the blessed, life-filled words which we see on the page, and mouth for the saying, and hear in the air; and in the mortal bodies of our baptized sisters and brothers with whom we share these pews, this sacred space.

And there is the *world on weekdays* embodiment. Again and again in the gospels, our Lord insists in word and gesture that he is bonded with human beings—with their ventures, their sufferings, and their joys: he insists, in fact, that he is embodied in us. When we give a cup of water to some thirsty person, we give it to him; when we visit a sick or a trapped person, we visit him; when we rejoice at anything good whatever, we rejoice with him—we are, in fact, an expression of his rejoicing.

So our feast today looks back with wonder and gratitude at the incarnation, the *embodiment*, of God among us at a particular moment of human history; and it looks around this chapel at the embodied selves, limping or sprightly, old or new, to be found here, as all of us

## Bread for the Journey

join to welcome Christ once more into our shared life; and it looks outwards at the wounded, yearning, process-filled body of the world. As we take the bread and wine, the Body and the Blood, let us rejoice at what God has done, and take heart for what there is yet to do.

*Newman: June, 1996*

SAINTS

# Hill and Valley
**All Saints**

MOST OF THE CHURCH'S FEAST-DAYS HAVE TO DO with one or two saints, or no more than a handful at most. But today's feast celebrates the whole bang lot of them, ancient and modern, men and women, smart and stupid, the long and the short and the tall, those we know about and those only God knows about. These people were dear to God, as we all are; they also, bit by bit, adopted God as dear to them: and this they did in the course of making others dear to them. Becoming holy is a process of endearment: and today we remember and acclaim all of those in whom this has happened.

Such a feast can bring out the best in an artist: in a musician, for instance, looking to celebrate the words of 'For All the Saints', or the words of 'When the Saints Go Marching In', and looking to celebrate the event itself. And then there are the many, many paintings and sculptures of golden beings, or figures done in ebony and oak and sandstone and marble. They crowd the pages of precious manuscripts and of throwaway pamphlets: they are reared on the walls of great cathedrals, and they are mocked up on the shelves of religious shops and shrines. They make a fine band, and it can do the heart good to think about them.

As we think about them, we thank God for them—we do that in every Mass of every saint—and we seek their support. And we have the best of warrants for asking that support, which is the combination of their love and our need. If they had not loved, they would not have been saints: there is no other way to become one. You can't apply to become a saint, asking for Special Consideration in that you were too busy to love, or too something else: the Examiner will not be satisfied. Anyhow, there they are, vindicated for ever in such attempts at love as they made. That vindication itself equips them, so to speak, to persist in their policy of compassion: and when we pray to them for help, we are appealing to their best and truest selves.

That is their love: but there is also our need. In the Gospel passage that we heard, the very familiar 'Beatitudes' or 'Blessings', there is a detail we might remember. St Matthew tells us that when our Lord saw how big the crowd was, he went up on a hill to speak to them. Well, if he was up on the high ground, they were down on the lower ground. And those people on the lower ground stand for all the saints in their passage through life: they stand for all of us, in our passage through life.

Traditionally, being 'lower down' stands for vulnerability and need. We do not think that the low man or low woman on a totem pole, metaphorically speaking, is doing very well: and when a former prime minister of this country described his opponents as 'pretty low down in the food chain', nobody took this as a compliment. Historically, when a rare few in Europe could afford to buy or breed and keep horses, the achieved height helped to give them power: and in time, some of them were actually called, 'Your highness'. We want to rise, not to fall.

But if we are realistic, we know that in many respects we stay 'low'. We are kept 'low', kept from being too cocky for too long, by many blunt realities: by our need for food and drink and sleep, all of them frequently; by our imperfectly met yearnings and aspirations, our re-drawn plans; by our sheer bafflement about so much of what goes on; by guilty memories and stubborn fears. All the fine talk in the world will not take us clear of these things: they are that very human condition which Jesus himself embraced, and, strangely, honoured by his presence.

We are people of the valley, of the lowlands. But so was each man, woman and child whom the Church honours today: and so are many others in whose hearts the grace of God is at work, hour after hour, week after week. And so indeed was Jesus to be. His stay on that hill was a brief one; he had a longer stay to make on the other hill of Calvary, and the valley of death to visit, all alone. Yet from his consenting to that low, and lowering, state, all the vigour to transform humanity, person by person and tribe by tribe, flowed. It continues to flow today, as we notice when we move towards the fortifying divine Bread and divine Wine. The Master of the Feast has good words for us too, good food to go with the words. Let us pray, one for another, to have hearts open to both: and so, with all the saints, to begin to move to glory.

*Newman: November, 1998*

**CHRIST THE KING**

# The Shepherd on the Cross

## Christ, Universal King, Year C

IF, WHEN YOU LEAVE THE CHAPEL TODAY BY THE main entrance, you turn to your left and look back towards the sacristy, you will see, beyond the tall metal gate and a few trees, a more-than-life-size figure of Christ. He is done in mild steel, he is pinned high up on a wall of the chapel, and he is gazing out, past trees and gate, towards Swanston Street. He might have been put there just for today's Feast of Christ the Universal King.

In the first of today's readings, we are reminded that King David, great ancestor of Jesus, was a crowned shepherd. Shepherds were not, in Israel, figures of glamour—in fact, in our Lord's time, they were not allowed to give witness in court, since the assumption was that under pressure they would lie. They were, shall we say, earthy: but they were also vital figures in the economy, and there was no substitute for them in the work that needed doing. If the shepherd did not look after the sheep, that was the end of the sheep.

It was such a man who was made 'the shepherd of Israel'. A people in need, turbulent within and beleaguered without, was given the custodian it needed—someone canny, someone earthy, but also someone visionary when it came to the people's deepest needs. He knew, as we say, more than his prayers; he was, while king, among other things an adulterer and a murderer; but somehow he could himself be shepherded by God back from these black-sheep ways, and resume the care of a people on their way to that same God.

Now remember that Jesus had not read some expurgated version of the scriptures, the legitimating document of his community of faith. He knew far better than we are likely to do the flaws in David's personality and the blots on his record. And yet, when he speaks of himself as 'good shepherd', he aligns himself with his ancestor. He says, in effect, that the truly regal, the truly authoritative thing about him is that, come what may, he will not give up on the sheep. In Jesus' case, it is the sheep, not the shepherd, that show the flaws; but either way, and for better or for worse, for richer or for poorer, in sickness and in health, he is theirs.

All of us, I suppose, have heard the expression, 'come hell or high water'. It comes from the American cattle-drives, over so many hundreds of miles, with millions of cattle driven that way. The 'hell' refers to the hellish heat that cattle and custodians had to survive together: the 'high water' refers to all the rivers that had, at some peril, to be swum. By the same token, Christ, our shepherd, is in it with us come hell or high water—through whatever personal or shared onerousness comes our way: through the shrivelling of the years, through the afflictive terrors. Most of us hear 'The Lord is my shepherd' principally, I suppose, at funerals: but there he is, our shepherd, in the bright days as in the dark ones—food-giver, drink-provider, as indeed at this very Eucharist.

But what has this to do with the figure on the wall, a few yards out there? Remember what our Gospel passage told us. There, the one who is labelled, in mockery, 'King of the Jews'—or, as we might say, 'Regal Shepherd'—this one is appealed to by someone who is exposed to the hell of crucifixion and the dark, high-mounting waters of death. The bandit or terrorist or freedom-fighter or whatever he was pleads to be shepherded beyond the filth and shame and despair of his appalling situation, and is told by the Shepherd-King that, yes, this will be done. The dying shepherd takes the dying sheep with him, a keeper of faith to the last.

That Lord Jesus is not some idol, however handsome, pinned as metal to courses of stone: the Lord Jesus truly re-presents himself in

## Bread for the Journey

this ceremony to us men and women of flesh and blood. Our company, as we believe, is his company; our food is of his feeding: in the words we have heard, and will hear, we catch the note of his voice. And yet I would invite you to spare a glance at Nickolaus Seffrin's sculpture, outside on the wall. There, the all-but-naked Jesus gazes, night and day, towards the secular bustle of Swanston Street, and Carlton, and all the vista beyond, across the sprawl of Melbourne. He watches, as shepherds must, and at cost to themselves, over a city's needs and a world's. And secondly, he gazes east. He gazes, as both churches and their believing communities are meant to do, towards sunrise, towards resurrection. He is the shepherd on the cross: and he shepherds us to that country where, at last, we shall be able to see every cross as a crook of love.

*Newman: November, 1995*

ASSUMPTION

# *Blessings in Disguise*
## Assumption of Mary

THE ACTOR ALEC GUINNESS WROTE AN AUTObiography called *Blessings in Disguise*. That title referred in part to the whole affair of being an actor— an occupation in which one is always, by definition, 'disguised' as someone else. But more importantly it referred to Guinness's view that many blessings in his life had come in the guise, in the costume, of something else—of something neutral, or of something distressing. Time was to tell, he implied, that these events, or encounters, or deprivations, were really blessings.

I mention this because our Gospel passage, which includes that prayer of praise of Our Lady's which is called the 'Magnificat', shows her as exulting in blessings in disguise. In just the way that her Son, later, was to use, she names various states of vulnerability and dependency, and says that she and others like her have been blessed just there. 'He has raised the lowly', she says: 'he has given the hungry every good thing.'

The place to start with such a celebration is, surely oneself. Telling other people how fortunate they are, when that is not how they see and feel things, is usually not a fruitful policy. There is an Irish saying which goes, 'It's easy to lie on another man's wound': glibness about the fortunes and the misfortunes of others is never a good idea. And there is nothing to suggest that our Lady was glib in that way, or in any other way: God knows, if anyone was to be aware of terrible suffering and deprivation, she was. Her warrant for speaking of blessings received by others was her singular readiness to attest the divine light which could reach her in darkness, the divine sweetness which could reach her in bitterness.

And if she has one thing more than another to teach us today, surely this is it: that growth in humanity, growth in the Spirit, begins and is fostered just where we thank God for our blessings. Our blessings, after all, include absolutely everything that has done us good, or can ever do us good. They include the discovery of fire and the invention of the alphabet and cookery and computers and snow and beaches and music and the Great Barrier Reef and every human intellectual discipline and smiles and the carpentry that made the benches we sit on, and all the rest of it.

More intimately still, blessings include each other, and they include ourselves. We came, each of us, from the nothingness which did not yield up those many siblings we might have had and will never have: and we are sustained in being at all from instant to instant not by some act of will of our own, or by the world's forces and powers alone, but by the empowering vitality of God himself. This is a blessed day for us—as are they all. As the darkness falls away at dawn, the masked blessing of the world, and of the life we live in it, is shown once more through its disguise.

Even more than that, though, what has brought us to this chapel, to this 'Eucharist' or Thanksgiving, is the greatest of blessings in disguise. We share a belief that the short life and pitiful death of Jesus the Unique One were vindicated in his resurrection. From the beginning of its existence, the Church has reiterated this; and without this, it has nothing of interest or importance to say at all: 'if Christ is not risen, our believing is empty'. We know from the gospels how drained and dismayed and disheartened the disciples of Jesus were when their stripped Lord was tortured to death: and how inhuman they would have been, if they had not been like that! We also know that what put heart into them again was not some passage of time, time the supposed 'great healer', but life's embracing, and being embraced anew by, that same Jesus. And we know besides that they did not thereupon forget about the suffering and only talk about the rising.

They insisted on the fact that it was in Christ's readiness to love to the end, how-ever odious that end, that definitive love was released into the world, of which the rising was the display. That is truly a case of blessings in disguise, and of blessings showing through. This is why we are here. And this is why, with the Mary who was uniquely open to being blessed, we make a feast of today.

*Newman: December, 1999*

ORDINARY TIME

# Lord of the Motley Array

### 3rd Sunday in Ordinary Time, Year B

MY BROTHERS AND SISTERS, AS YOU WILL HAVE noticed, in the Church's way of calculating these things, we are back once more in 'Ordinary Time'—this being the third Sunday of that period. When I was a raw young trainee Jesuit, I walked for the first time into the common room in which much of my life was to be lived for a couple of years, and I saw on the notice-board, in Latin, a description of the order of events. I was jumpy, and my Latin was sketchy, so I read the timetable as announcing that certain things were to be done, '... until death'. It wasn't really as bad as all that. The real message was that they were to be done until 'ordinary time' took over. And so it has, for all of us, once again.

What are we to make of 'ordinary time?' Personally, I think that one of the blessings provided by the arts of the secular world for at least a couple of hundred years has been the thoroughness with which it has taken 'ordinary time' seriously. The novel, the film, much poetry, painting, music, essay-writing and journalism, sculpture—they have produced torrents of rubbish, of course, as human beings do every day and always have done, but they have become very inventive and insightful in showing us that the ordinary is not necessarily the forgettable. They have, in other words, been celebrating Ordinary Time, in all its motley array.

I use this last expression deliberately, and am prompted to do so by elements from today's readings: but before I come to them, a word about another point of reference. Looking at a Jesuit work of reference which alludes to those who have died, in Australia, and thus have claims on the prayers of living Jesuits, I notice the names of those who died yesterday, and today, and tomorrow. About today's couple, I cannot speak, since I never knew them: but of yesterday's, and tomorrow's, I can certainly claim that they were part of a motley array. All of them were good men; some of them were odd men: and you could have written an interesting essay or short story about any one of them, after half an hour's acquaintance with him. They were, in other words, normal, standard, human beings—they were part of the motley array.

You could club them in, for instance, with the little bunch of apostles-to-be who are referred to in today's Gospel: and in one or two cases, you could club them in, with no trouble at all, with the Jonah of our first reading—the prophet who is told to go and preach in a large, recalcitrant city, and who is remarkably and repeatedly stroppy when things don't go as he has expected. One feature of these dead good men, my fellow Jesuits, as it seems to me, is that they expected, on the whole, that things would proceed according to prescribed patterns; but they then adjusted, according to their capacities, when the patterns were revised or broken. I am reminded of a hand-lettered notice which I saw in a Jesuit house in Paris a year or so ago. It said that if there was 'a catastrophe' with the washing-machine, then one should consult Father So-and-so. We all have catastrophes: and usually there isn't, in the full sense, a Father So-and-so to consult; and yet in some scarred and patched degree we find that we come good, by God's grace, in our coping with life's mottled array.

Our Lord lived most of his time in 'Ordinary Time'; and so did our Lady; and so have all the countless millions of women and men who have tried to follow the shifting light of grace which has come their way, day by day, and year by year, throughout their lives. It has always been a bit of a mess: often, it has been mainly a mess. By contrast with the sacred paintings, reproduced in their millions, not a single person, from Jesus the Lord down, has ever walked through life with a halo or other badge of divine endorsement about them. He was, his mother was, the apostles all were, walking in Ordinary Time: and it was out of that faithful walking, as we believe, that all the good of all the world germinated and came to fruit and flower. Perhaps that is something for all of us, too, to remember tomorrow (which is the feast of St Francis de Sales), and the next day (which is the feast of the Conversion of St Paul), and the next day, Wednesday (which is Australia Day.) Every motley Australian has a stake in Ordinary Time, the time in which God's eternal stake in all of us comes home.

*Newman: January, 2000*

# SEASONS

AUTUMN

# *The Lord of Autumn*

WE HAVE LIVED EACH DAY OF OUR LIVES IN SOME season or other, and we always will do so. True, at points of extremity on our globe, equator or pole, the fluctuations are minimized; but even there, the seasons matter, and greatly. Wherever we live, we can, essentially, do no more about the seasons than we can about day and night, for all our bufferings and elaborate adjustments. What we can do is accommodate ourselves to them, going with their promises and not being daunted by their demands.

And so it goes with the life of our spirits, our hearts. There is no aseasonal existence for them either. Under a wide array of influences, only a few of which any of us can identify with accuracy, we find ourselves in conditions which correspond to the shifts of the natural world. If we are not to settle for being merely embattled, or merely cynical, we have to learn, and relearn, to identify providential aspects in what we are undergoing.

We can be confused in this venture by the fact that there is often little apparent synchronization between my season and yours. You are riding high, to all outward seeming, whereas I am at best slogging along in the mud: or you, after a bad run, are coming good, while I am tilting downwards, and can't find the brake. It sounds, in fact, rather like many episodes in the gospels, when our Lord's reading and experience of a given situation is notably different from that of his followers. Not everything has changed since those first months and years.

When it is autumn in Melbourne, people often speak well of it, preferring it in fact to any other season. The days can be both crisp and bright, the fallen leaves are not yet so much soggy mulch, and the memory of summer is still there, warming and gentled, both. But we all know where autumn is headed: and we know that all that leaf-shedding is part of nature's strategy for the very survival of the trees. Autumn is what might be called the season of mixed blessings.

In the same way, we may hope to turn to the Lord of Autumn as the Lord of mixed blessings. Something, in many of us, hankers to have things straightened out, to have the contrasting elements of life put into distinguishable and unconfused piles. And this wish, or ideal, or whatever it is, has often been intensified by the voice of Christian teachers, local or remote, who call upon us not to make compromises, not to cut deals with tempters or cajolers, whoever they may be. If we are to live aptly as Christians, we may feel, surely the Lord ought keep things clear for us.

But while sometimes he does, sometimes he doesn't. 'Lord I believe, help thou my unbelief' might have been the prayer not only of the distressed parent, and not only of a Thomas awash in his doubts, but of any Christian ancient or modern, man woman or child. Our Lord's own, 'If it be possible, let this cup not come to me: still, if you want it, I will take it', is the prayer of someone who is himself under the providence of a shadowed Father. The preacher who had spoken of weeds among the wheat, of edible and inedible fish, came many times into situations in which half-formed hearts were half-offered to him, and half withheld.

We are told that our Lord 'learned obedience in suffering', and one of the sufferings was the requirement that he live in autumns of the spirit. In the couple of thousand years during which known or anonymous artists have been representing him and his doings, they have very frequently shown him as lodged amidst intricacies, as partly displayed and partly undisplayable. This is quite the opposite of being in some situation of moral shiftiness, in which there is always room to back off, or to move sideways: there was no backing off the cross, and the only ones at his side were themselves men brought to book. But it is fair to say that one condition of our Lord's being schooled to be our heroic saviour was that he keep his spiritual nerve in the mingled circumstances of life, whether life outside or life inside.

'The servant is not greater than the master', and we too may expect that a good deal of our Christian living will be autumnal living. The Church's longest stretch of its liturgical year is not the Lent of penitence, nor the Easter of exuberance, but the 'Ordinary Time' in which we will or will not become saints. We may hope to have all sorts of comrades on this way: each of them can be backed by the Lord of autumn.

*Newman: May, 1995*

ELECTIONS

# *Power, Love, Wisdom*
## 27th Sunday in Ordinary Time, Year C

YESTERDAY, AS YOU ALL KNOW, WE HAD ourselves an election, the object of which was to put a certain group of people, as we say, 'into power'. And that indeed is the truth of it. Easily, or with difficulty, these men and women can make laws by which we will all be bound, and determine policies by which we will all be affected. That is power: and whether or not we think about it, we may be sure that our political servants think about it—some of them, night and day.

Often we are suspicious of power and of the powerful, and that is healthy enough. But power is like, say, human sexuality or the human mind: it is a great gift which can be used splendidly or can be misused horribly. It is not good that people in general should be powerless: it is good that most people, most of the time, should be empowered.

I mention this because it is part of St Paul's theme in the reading which we have just heard. He assures his hearers that the Spirit of God is one who offers power. And my first stress is on the fact that all the 'powers' we have, whether they are physical or mental or emotional or social or anything else, are effects of God's action among us. As we waxed from our fragile condition in the womb, through the frailty of infancy and childhood, to wherever we are now, we were being made gifts daily, in the power to speak, or to

*Often we are suspicious of power and of the powerful, and that is healthy enough. But power is like, say, human sexuality or the human mind: it is a great gift which can be used splendidly or can be misused horribly.'*

walk, or to decide, or to relate, or to flourish in any fashion at all. We speak of power-dressing, of power-walking: but all of us have been dressed in power, have been empowered to walk, on more days than we can possibly remember. The God we call 'all-powerful' uses that power to flood our lives with the skills, and energies, and enthusiasms, which keep us vital and on the go.

Which is all very fine: but we know well enough that this can go awry. There is a saying, 'the bigger they are, the harder they fall', and people have been saying that kind of thing for thousands of years, because those rich in one kind of power or another have so often abused it. Immensely clever people have done immense good, and immense harm: great charm and beauty have broken hearts, and homes, and hopes: enthusiasms for tribes and states and flags have covered the acres with graves. So it is not surprising that St Paul also says that God's Spirit is the giver of love: God help us all when we are in the hands of the powerful and unloving, for that is the devil's territory.

And since the Scripture is not intended simply for our interested inspection, but is meant to alter our lives, any of us might well ask how lovingly, how generously, we exercise our powers, whatever they are. We are, you see, not the absolute owners of these, any more than our politicians 'own' power. Power is lent them so that they can do good on our behalf: powers are lent us so that we can do good on one another's behalf. Your ability to interest other people, or to persuade them, or to impress them, are precious things, but they are not meant to be hoarded to yourself, as in old legends dragons guarded hoards of gold. Your intellectual skills or sporting prowess or sociability come from God's hand each day, like the sun's light and consciousness itself, for the betterment of those you meet or contact, near or far. It is to open hands, not to hoarding hands, that the greatest gifts come.

The third thing St Paul says about the giving Spirit is that wisdom, too, is in the Spirit's gift. We are supposed to keep our wits about us when trying to play our part in the world. C. S. Lewis said of some well-intentioned woman, 'She went around doing good to others: you could tell the others by their hunted look'. The greater the need we are trying to address, the more thoughtfully, the more wisely, we will need to bring our powers to bear, whatever they may be. Just as we try not to elect idiots to govern us, we try not to let idiots determine or influence the run of our ordinary days. But usually what's in question is not stark choices between evident sense and evident idiocy, but a somewhat complex, frequently-changing, state of affairs. One of the things that a university can do for us is to help us reflect on that complexity, and to be insightful about it. That, too, is something done by virtue of God's empowering Spirit, though you won't find much acknowledgement of that in most Australian universities. But whatever you think of universities, or of politicians, you might pray once more at this Mass for the divine gift of wisdom to all of them. They do need it, after all: and so do we.

*Newman: 1998*

## AUSTRALIA DAY

# Blessed Australia
### Australia Day

A COUPLE OF DAYS AGO WE CELEBRATED Australia Day, a festival prompted by the raising of the British flag in Sydney Cove on 26 January, 1788. The event has become contentious, but whatever of that, an event it certainly was: and it is extremely unlikely that any of us would be here today unless it had taken place.

Frequently, when people compare that moment with similar earlier moments in North America, a contrast is made between the ethos of the Australian 'First Fleet' and the ethos of the so-called 'Pilgrim Fathers'. It is said that religion, for good or for ill, animated the English travellers who were on their way to becoming Americans: whereas religion, in the gaolers or the gaoled, was at best incidental in the Australian moment. What we can say with some confidence is that, so far as the native Americans or the native Australians were concerned—the people who had been on their continents for much longer than there were identifiable European countries—the newcomers who waded ashore did not look much like emissaries from heaven. Indeed, they must have seemed to be, as they quickly proved to be, very bad news indeed for the ancient inhabitants of these enormous regions.

I am noting this, not to get into some argument about colonialism or land rights, but prompted by today's Gospel, which we have just heard, and which, unflinchingly, speaks about the terms of blessedness, of a happy condition, of something to make the heart beat faster. What on earth, do you suppose, could Governor Phillip, or his toughened officers, or his dislocated prisoners, or whatever local inhabitant may have skirted the bay—what could such people possibly have made of that refrain which we sometimes call 'The Beatitudes', the 'All-Flooding Blessings'? Out they spill, these improbable claims: 'Blessed are the poor in spirit, and the sorrowing, and those hungry and thirsty for holiness, and the merciful, and the single-hearted, and the peacemakers, and the slandered'. If anyone, then and there, had heard such improbabilities, surely they would at best have kept a poker-face, and grown impatient until this devout charade was over. Sydney, in January, is not very pleasant even now, and it cannot have done much for devotion in the scourging time of 1788.

We cannot go back to their situation: our imagining of it is at best costume-drama, and we seem to see the camera for some miniseries dollying about the troubled scene. But isn't there something which we do indeed have in common with any such imaginable group—a hesitancy, namely, about the words which may, at best, have been dragged out of our Lord—dragged out, because he had been around for the bulk of a lifetime in almost as unforgiving a country as Australia, and under a foreign occupation which in the end spoke only the language of the sword?

Never forget that Jesus Christ spent the whole of his life in a country under foreign occupation. The Roman Empire (as it had become during his time) could be cooperative when this was in its interest, could cut deals, could establish taxation franchises as, nowadays, franchises for McDonalds are established, could delegate administration to whatever local collaborators were skilled at that kind of thing. But the bottom line, for the Empire, was always power, and money its instrument and token: the bottom line was readiness to break the vulnerable, to seduce the single-hearted, to carve through the ranks of the peacemakers, to defame and debase those who might promote integrity to the last. The Empire did what empires do: it believed in nothing beyond its own identity and its own resources. It adored itself.

# Bread for the Journey

Another way of putting this is to say that it was terrified, as empires always come to be. On the one hand it kept on singing its own praises—boosting the Eagles, invoking its own magical name, strutting and thundering: on the other hand, it could not come to terms with its own absolute vulnerablity, with the fact that it was of course crucified to its own mortality. It was like sundry other empires, earlier and later: Troy's, Babylon's, China's, Portugal's, England's, America's. It was made of brick-dust: and when the brick-work was cracked, the dust all bled away.

There is no particular reason to suppose that when our Lord proclaimed the blessings he would foster, he was, so to speak, behaving like an Australian, and cutting down the tall poppies—'goodbye Babylonians, Romans, Americans'. Rather, he was cherishing those great forms of spiritual creativity which can be deployed in or out of any empire, in or out of any democracy or autocracy or aristocracy. He was, without any illusions whatever, singing the praises, not of moral opportunists, but of spiritual visionaries—the non-adapters, the un-realists, as the imperialists would think.

Much later, in our own almost-done-with twentieth century of the Lord, another brooding Jew, Franz Kafka, would say, 'The good is victorious, but not in this world'. Jesus, our Lord, thinking of the peace-makers and the seekers of authenticity, and the hungerers for outright goodness, would agree with Kafka. It is not in this world that the good is victorious, but victorious it is: and God help any of us who have, by contrast, cast our lot in with the doomed cause of crookedness.

*Newman: January, 1996*

ANZAC

# *Anzac Day and Easter*

IT SAYS IN THE BOOK OF DIRECTIONS FOR SAYING Mass here that 'Anzac Day is not commemorated liturgically today'. That may be so, but it would be a strange thing, and an unfortunate thing, if we did not have Anzac Day in mind as we gather. There are a couple of reasons why this is so.

The first is that, in Australian civil society, this is about as special a day as we have. And if you believe, as I do, that God's Holy Spirit works to bring about distinctive moral and spiritual awarenesses in each country, then you will want us to be alert to whatever it is that tugs at memory, and imagination, and emotion, and reflective intelligence, on such a day as this. If Australians are right to find value in Anzac Day, it is God who makes them right. So people of specifically Christian allegiance should not be casual about it, much less dismissive. After all, it is our business to try to go where he shows himself, rather than demanding that he attend where we choose to be.

The other reason for us to remember Anzac Day, to remember all of those from our country who have lived or died in war, and those who have been affected by that living and dying, is this: in some measure this is where we all are. I don't want to be glib about the matter—glibness would be offensive, and foolish, both—but the truth is that to a greater or a lesser extent we are all part of the dark ecosystem of violence. We are accustomed to the notion that the physical world, from equator to the poles, is exposed to pollution—that filth in the rivers and foulness belched into the air does not stay just where it is discharged, but becomes a shared menace, a shared taint. In somewhat the same way, our minds and hearts can be tainted by the deadliness of conflict wherever it is to be found. People much like you and me, so far as we can tell, are doing dreadful things to one another, and having such things done to them, in more parts of the Earth than will fit easily on the front page of any newspaper. Once we knew of this only by rumour, and well after the event. These days, a cell-phone might tell us; or email, sent by a shaking hand; or a television image, courtesy of the bomber, and the bombed.

So when we gather, as we do now, to be explicitly a part of the living embodiment of Christ, we do well to remember, in all sobriety, that he said that whatever was done to the least of his human brothers (and sisters) was done to him. When, in this Mass, we come to commune with the Lord of all life, we are also communing with those in whose sufferings Christ himself, and life itself, are insulted. In this Mass, as at every Mass, we will pray for peace, a prayer uniquely apt on Anzac Day: and in doing so, we are certainly not praying for an abstraction. We are praying that the divine pity may have entrance into human hearts, today, now, this moment.

If we are genuine about this, and if we take seriously our Lord's claim in today's Gospel that he has come so that we may have life, and life to the full, surely we must ask whether there is an Anzac Cove in our own hearts, a Gallipoli of animus, of frank loathing or smouldering resentment. It is true that some things are hateful—my own list of them is not a small one—but no person is hateful. Hatred of any person, public or private, fouls the air of the heart and the spirit. By contrast, every gesture of forgiveness and reconciliation works to freshen that shared atmosphere. It was by just such a largesse of heart that Christ our Lord saved us from nullity and futility—from some eternal unmarked grave. As we receive his living presence together today, may we be readied to offer it to anyone who will have it from us.

*Newman: April, 1999*

OLYMPIC GAMES

# *The Self at Play*

THE MOST IMPORTANT THING ABOUT GAMES IS that they are useless. Learned and intelligent books have been written, especially in this century, about this fact. Games, play—they are there for their own sweet sake. People who love chess play it not to pass time, or to heighten their alertness to life's complexity, but in order to be in chess's world, that land of liberty and constraint. People who, as we say, *play* music, do it in order to go to the land of harmony. When Shakespeare wrote plays, he did it to relish, and help others to relish, the possibilities of the imagination.

That is what all play is about: it is what the poet Yeats calls 'life's own self-delight'. Of course play, like anything else, can be turned to other purposes. When a Russian Grand Master meets an American in a chess tournament, there is going to be more than chess at issue, in the public mind. When one city out-bids another to attract a great conductor to its podium, there is more than melody on its mind. When Shakespeare wrote the plays, he was also making a living.

But at its heart, play is like love, or like prayer: one does it because it is a good thing, whether or not there is any discernible gain from it. Certainly, feeling the point of going on loving, or going on praying, can wane. Love can be rejected, abused, ignored; and after a while, it seems just too stressful to persist with it. Prayer can seem to be just a noise in the void—what Hopkins called 'dead letters sent to dearest him who lives, alas, away'. So we get out of the way of loving or of praying, and get on with something else that seems to have a yield to it, something still treasurable.

Still, people do come back to love, come back to prayer. We can relearn the knack of it, re-acquire the taste for it. It's like getting back onto a bicycle when one hasn't been on one for years; there is a moment of wobbling, but then the skill returns, and the gladness to be there. People speak sometimes of a 'second journey' in life, which may take the form of a new relationship, a new career, a new policy or attitude towards the years yet to come. We can make second journeys into love, second journeys into prayer. When we do, we are likely to prize the loving or praying condition even more than was possible during the 'first journey'.

I think of these matters when watching or listening to the Olympic Games. God knows, there is plenty wrong with them. The drugs, discovered or undiscovered; the cutthroat manoeuvering for franchises, the strident nationalism, the fetishism of Gold: this is all cheerless stuff. But buried underneath it all, and dug up by some every day, is a joy in the disciplined exercise of the body, this marvellous thing which we are and aren't entirely. It is the body at play, and the relishing self at play, that justifies the Games, as it does all games.

It is an excellent thing that so many millions of people throughout the world are in sympathy with the Games. In other circumstances, we are bonded by other things, some of them melancholy. Whether or not we do anything, or can do anything, about natural or man-made disasters, we resonate with distress, even if passing distress, when we know of them. Sometimes, at moments of crisis, it is as if the whole world is afflicted with a virus of anxiety—as during what, for the first time in history, were called 'World Wars'. By contrast, a shared enthusiasm for the Games at their best, even while we wince at them when they are at their worst, is something to rejoice in.

Is this mere distraction from our problems, a diversion which is unbecoming in adults? In part, no doubt, it is. Show me someone who always uses everything in the right way, and I will show you, not a saint, but an angel. But the good of the Games is more than their

'Except for the bed-bound, I must be
the least Olympian Jesuit in Australia.
But the Games have plenty to teach me:
something about solidarity, something about
relish, something about prayer, something
about love. It is not a bad hand, for people
moving their bodies through space.'

value as diversion. They contain, in a summary way, much that we value when anything is being done for its own sake, and done *well*. The real triumph of the Games is not that some few come first, but that all do well, and in spite of the strain and the pain, relish what they are doing.

There is a saying, 'The best is the enemy of the good'; Chesterton said, 'If a thing is worth doing, it is worth doing badly'. What both sayings are getting at, by exaggerating, is the truth that accomplishments are real even when—as usual—they are not conquests. It is easy for us to lose sight of this fact. Ours is a rather jumpy, competitive society, where it is easy for us to dismiss one another as not up to scratch. If we like to cut down the tall poppies, the middle-sized poppies too, and even the seedlings, can have a bad time of it. 'Winning', said a famous American coach, 'isn't the main thing. It's the only thing'. That's a lie, but it's a lie believed from time to time by many Australian men, women, and children.

Except for the bed-bound, I must be about the least Olympian Jesuit in Australia. But the Games have plenty to teach me: something about solidarity, something about relish, something about prayer, something about love. It is not a bad hand, for people moving their bodies through space.

*Newman: August, 1992*

RUNNING THE RACE

## *The Run*

### 20th Sunday in Ordinary Time, Year C

SOMETIMES, WHEN WE LISTEN TO THE WORDS OF the Bible, or read them, we may wonder who they were written for: or at least, we may feel that they're not written for us. The context sounds foreign, and so do the stories, and even the bottom line can sound pretty odd. There are reasons for all that, and from time to time we do need the active foreign-ness: it can give us a bit of a jolt, and help us to change our minds. But the reading we all heard today, the reading from what is called the 'Letter to the Hebrews', is not like that. It might in fact have been tailor-made for Australians. It is all about the dynamics of athletic competition.

There's no major news session on the radio or on television which does not pay attention to the ways in which Australians are making their run. They may be doing it on a football field, or over hurdles, or in a marathon, or in a hundred-metres' dash, or in some variant on all these things, but we assume that they'll be having a go. And even those of us who are too old or too slow or too busy to be having that kind of go can have our hearts lifted when we watch the others, or hear about them.

This is a very old story among human beings—at least several thousand years old. So when the writer of the letter which we have just heard being re-read talks about all of us as being runners-in-life, he may be be writing in a foreign language, in a foreign place, and in an ancient time, but he is basically telling our story, singing our song.

The letter-writer says at one point, 'let us keep our eyes on Jesus, who both inspires us and rounds off our efforts in belief'. He doesn't say this glibly. When he writes this, he is, as you and I are at this moment, in the thick of life's demands. He knows that there is an array of things to be dealt with—some of them provided by the way the world is at large, some of them pressed on us by the whole complex of our relationships, and some of them thrown up just by the fact that I am myself—male or female, young or not so young, skilled or floundering, confident or doubtful. In other words, the letter-writer knows that when we are making our run in life, each of us does it with some complexity.

And there is another point. Since he is not stupid, this letter-writer knows that each of us is making the run for the first time. I'm different from my parents, different from my children, if I have any: I'm different from my brother or sister, and from the person next to me in the pew at the moment. I'm a one-off. I can get cues, or clues, from people who've gone before me, or from my contemporaries: but I'm the absolutely first, and the absolutely last, person who will make my particular run.

Now this is fine as long as my run is going well, but it can be disconcerting when the going is tough. Fear can snarl at us, depression can drag our hearts down, regret can darken our horizon, guilt can knock the spirit out of us. But what I have to say to you now, my sisters and brothers in fragility, is that it is exactly to us, the vulnerable ones, that this word of God is addressed. Elsewhere, our Lord says very frankly, in effect, 'it is when you are sick—first, last, always—that you have a claim on me'. And in fact, it is because all of humanity, in the past and in the present and in any conceivable future, suffers the ills of mortality, that Jesus came, and came to stay.

Whenever I make my run in life, if I am running in the way I identify as most genuine, there will be a shadowy runner at my side, and that will be not my shadow, but God's shadow, the shadow of Jesus. Every time I am patient and tender, though impatience and hostility nag at me, the shadow of God and of Jesus will also be there.

*Seasons*

If I go, not just an extra mile, but an extra yard or two on somebody else's behalf, this will not after all be something trivial, but will be, in effect, the throwing of that shadow of God and of Jesus in front of me. When there are pressures to fake things in my relationships or to bluff in my studies or to play the child in an adult world, and I resist those pressures, this too will not just be a matter of my putting on a good moral performance: it will be a moment in which God will put his hand on my backbone and at my heart, and will urge me forward, with all those I love, towards the fullest of all lives.

It is true that we doubt these things, again and again. It is true that very soon all of us, you and I and all the rest of us, will go out of this religious theatre, this chapel, and will have to resume the threads of life. But what I am saying to you, and what is said to you dramatically when you eat the bread of God and drink the wine of God, is that the word of God which you have heard is no merely dreamy matter, no little religious fantasy for a few minutes in the midst of the week's hours. You can decide how you will live your life. Nobody can decide this for you. Nobody *will ever* have a chance to do it really well in exactly the way you can do it really well. This *is* the time of your personal best, and there is no second time for it. If there is somebody who is haunting you while you think about it, perhaps it is God who is the haunter.

*Newman: August, 1995*

MOTHER'S DAY

# God's Comfort

WE ARE GIVEN CUES, INCESSANTLY AS IT sometimes seems, about comfort. We are asked whether we are comfortable in shoes we are perhaps about to buy, or in suits, or dresses. We are asked whether we are comfortable with various opinions, or attitudes, or stances. We are challenged about what are called our 'comfort zones', those psychic spaces within which we can manoeuvre easily, as an infant does within its play-pen. We are made comfortable for an interview, or for an encounter with a dentist, or for the sake of a challenge or a summons. Society, poor worried thing, consults us a lot about comfort.

Does comfort matter? I think that it does, but not precisely for the reasons held in mind by the people who usually ask us about it. Of course, as much as you do, I want my neck to be un-cricked on a long flight: and of course, as much as you do, I do not want to be surrounded by people with whose opinions or temperaments I am at odds. But what 'comfort' means, in its origins, is that condition in which one is not enfeebled: the real 'comfort zone' is the milieu of resourcefulness, of strength. To be *profoundly* comfortable is to be sustained and maintained from the base upwards, from the heart outwards.

Christianity is committed, entirely and permanently, to 'comfort' in that sense. It isn't committed to easy-going-ness: it is committed to sustaining and maintaining those energies and commitments without which we can never be at ease. The Lord Jesus said, variously, 'I have come to bring not peace but a sword,' and, 'The thing I use to yoke you with others is gentle: the thing I give you to carry is not crushing'. These sayings do not reflect, merely, the moods of Jesus, whatever they may have been; they reflect a sense that what we are called to be or do is an adult task, a task for which we are in fact all fitted, and which requires that we not behave in an infantile way, but which, once accepted, will both tax us and endorse our efforts.

In fact, Christianity—the good Word of the good Lord—tells us to grow up. I do not know, and I imagine that you do not know, what percentage of people have ever grown up, or have even planned to do so. It is easy for us to condescend to cultures in which girls' feet have been bound tightly lest they grow to normal human size: it is easy to condescend to circumstances in which people had, or have, little access to knowledge, which is always a sleeping power. True, it is odious that human beings should be deprived of opportunities to bud, to flower, to flourish. But, my sisters and brothers, who of us can say that, endowed with the gifts and the opportunities we enjoy, we have unambiguously been committed to growing up, and out, and in, and on? Remember what we said, every last one of us, at the beginning of this Eucharist, and think again. Each of us has a cowardly, ghostly shadow, which kisses the chains around each one's heart. There is a kind of diabolical brat which rides on your shoulders, rides on my shoulders, to say that none of us should ever grow up.

Is this a private fantasy of mine? No, it is not. We are told by God's Word that it was 'because of the Devil's envy' that death came into the world, that it was because of the Devil's envy that we should be courtiers of death rather than courtiers of life. 'The Devil's envy' is a succinct way of speaking of everything in our experience which begrudges human flourishing, which fosters gutlessness, which drips death into our veins. We have in Australia a way of talking about various unhappy developments in forests. It is called 'dieback.' Any useful talk about devils, or demons, or the diabolical, has to do with human dieback. Against all that, Jesus our disconcerted but resolute brother went to war—went to war to the utmost, so that all of us might, forever, not have dieback, but might live-forward.

The 'Spirit' of Jesus, the flying flame of his heart, is the One he promised to us, to brace us, to re-envigorate us, to keep the dream of flourishing alive and effective in our hearts too. It happens that today is Mothers' Day, a day on which we celebrate, fittingly, not only our mothers' tenderness and indispensable sweetness, but also their feeding into us all those resources which we needed, and need, to go on embracing life. In the Old Testament, the God who cherished us into life challenges us to deny whether he can be less loving than our mothers. So today, thanking that same God for our mothers, and our fathers, and the countless generations which have brought us to be, let us ask also for a fortified belief, an intensified and resolute and unflinching belief, in the God who wishes us well, and wishes us to grow, and wishes for all of us courage, generosity, and tenderness—the God who hates dieback, and loves each one of us with an enthusiasm compared with which every human enthusiasm is pale. Those are good things to ask for. And the God from whose womb each of us came is a good one from whom to ask it.

*Newman: May, 1996*

ALL HALLOWS

## *Halloween*

### 31st Sunday in Ordinary Time, Year A

TODAY, AS IT HAPPENS, IS BOTH THE 31ST SUNDAY of Ordinary Time, and the 31st of October. Our being so late in the series of Sundays is a hint that we are coming towards the shift into Advent: and our being on the 31st of October means that we are on what is called, in another hemisphere, 'Halloween'—which means, the evening of 'All Hallows', or as we would say, 'All Saints'.

Halloween means little or nothing to most of us, I imagine. If it means anything, it stands either for rather mindless horror movies or for tame fancy-dress parties laid on for children, with jagged faces cut in yellow North-American pumpkin-skins. But for hundreds of years, under another name, this day meant a great deal in, for instance, Ireland. It was the turning point into all the fiercenessness of a northern winter. It was marked by the slaughter and the drying or salting of cattle, for survival's sake in the months to come. It had more than a touch of looking over the brink of mortality about it. It was a day of perturbation—and indeed, it is out of that dimly-remembered perturbation that the modern flummery about ghosts and demons and witches, supposedly busy on this day, emerged.

I hope that we are not troubled by them: and indeed, I hope that the prayer that we say in every Mass, the prayer for peace in the world at large and in our hearts, is vindicated for each of us. But none of us was born yesterday, and each of us knows that, by night or by day, perturbations can rise in that world, and in those hearts. This is is a handsome chapel, which is why so many people want to be married in it, people whom we should always wish joy. But whoever they are, and however many of them there are, no celebrant will want to be shrouding the crucifix which, up there over the high altar, is a permanent presence. That crucifix stands indeed for divine love—if it did not, it would have no place here—but it stands for a divine love which is as rooted in the actualities of our lives as the cross had to be rooted in the earth to bear its singular burden. And what is true for so splendid a moment as a marriage ceremony is true too for our commonplace days, and our commonplace Sundays—as I dare say this one is for most of us: we need to be sponsored by the Lord of shifts and seasons, of sickness and health, of the better times and the worse times, of the rich days and the poor days. We need the warrant, and the memory, and self-staking, of no one less than God on the hours of our days and our nights.

And it is just this, happily, that is brought home to us once more in our readings today. All three of them speak the language of fathering and of mothering. Our first reading asks, rhetorically, 'Do we not have one Father?': St Paul claims, emphatically, to have all-but-suckled his Christian converts: Jesus insists again that the fatherhood of God pervades everything about us, whether or not we notice this. I know, and you know, that parents have problems with children, and children have problems with parents; on the record, so did our Lord with Mary and Joseph, and so he did with the followers whom he called 'children'. But when we come right down to it, this original, intimate, perpetual bond between parents and children is perhaps the most eloquent of all relationships. And what we have on offer today, at this hinge-moment of a festival, is the reminder that the God who begets us can never forget us: can never forget, does not want to forget, would not if he could. Today's readings help us to celebrate the fact that we are always on God's mind, and always in his heart.

Is he always on our mind, always in our hearts? You must answer for yourselves: but I dare guess not. Still, let us take heart from the reflection that tomorrow is the feast of those 'Hallows' I mention, is the Feast of All Saints. This means that it is a day resonant with the knowledge of all those good men and women who, like ourselves, have sprung, or limped, or scuttled, or waddled, by God's loving grace, into his definitive and deathless presence. In Ireland, those hundreds of years ago, as this day heralded the coming of a long and exacting chill, people made provision for life. In another country, in another world almost, we too make provision for life. We turn to the company of those who have the flavour and tang and perpetual presence of God about them—all those saints, named or unnamed. And we turn, whatever our weaknesses or follies or fears, to those like ourselves with whom, here and now, we celebrate this Eucharist. We are all the children of God: and he is not one to father in vain.

*Newman: October, 1999.*

DAILY BREAD

# The Man With the Fish and the Bread

### 3rd Sunday of Easter, Year C

A FEW YEARS AGO SOMEBODY WROTE A BOOK about the history of the fish-and-chips business. As with many other things, there's more involved in it all than you might originally suppose. But what any of us can easily do is recognize that eating fish and chips has a bit more to it than straight nourishment. It's warm and messy and casual, and it has a bonding quality about it: it seems better if you do it in company with other people.

In the Gospel we have just heard, our Lord doesn't offer his friends fish and chips—the potato wasn't to arrive from America for about another sixteen hundred years—but fish and bread, which comes to much the same sort of thing. The situation is about as down-to-earth as anyone could wish. The disciples have been fishing all night, which is hard work, and have caught nothing, which is bad news. Peter is stripped for action, and I suppose the others are too: and after a sleepless and fruitless night, and granted that they are an excitable bunch at the best of times, they can't be in the best of moods.

A man calls to them from the shore, with what sounds like an amateur's tip for a last throw of the net, and they find that it works, works to the point where they have more fish than they can handle. They lug it ashore as well as they can, with impetuous Peter having splashed on before them, and they find that Jesus is there, cooking

'... eating fish and chips has a bit more to it than straight nourishment. It's warm and messy and casual, and it has a bonding quality about it: it seems better if you do it in company with other people.'

them breakfast. It might have been fish and chips if the potato had arrived, but as it was, it was fish and bread—maybe toasted.

This, says St John, our Gospel-writer, is the third time that Jesus showed himself to the disciples after he had risen from the dead. In other words, although he had had plenty of practice at arranging food or drink for other people, this time something extra was at issue. He was showing them, once more, not only who he was, but also who he could be for them. The various pictures we have of the risen Jesus in the Gospels never offer him to us just as someone saying, 'Look, they killed me, but they couldn't keep a good man down': they never propose him to us as a boaster, though God knows, if you can beat death, that is something for people to notice in you. All of the Gospel stories about the risen Lord, and every Christian celebration of the risen Lord, like the Mass we are sharing in at this moment—all of these things insist that Jesus is the one who can change our whole orientation, can change the calibre and the quality of our whole lives, greatly to our advantage, if we will hear him and follow his words.

The ordinariness of the fish-and-bread is a reminder that the presence of God's energetic love is not something just for big-deal occasions, for the religious equivalent of Olympic Games or first nights at the Opera. We pray in every 'Our Father' for our daily bread—something as common as the unremarkable non-gourmet white stuff for which many of us have an appetite. Each of the Jesuits who has been helping to staff this College for the last seventy-seven years was trained in a tradition of looking for God in each of your faces, and through your gifts and needs, your ups and downs. This isn't so much because they were Jesuits as because they were Christians: they were trying to follow the logic of the good news of God as the one who comes to us in the daily bread of our lives. No doubt they did it, as they still try to do it, in the hope that this would be your purpose too.

When Christianity was an outlawed religion, near the time of its origins, Christians developed a verbal and visual code for talking about Christ and themselves. They called him The Fish, and they thought of themselves as people of The Fish. Apart from being good for us as part of the diet, fish just keep coming: there are billions of them at any particular moment. And to think of Jesus as the Fish, or as the Fish-person, is to think of him as the One who won't run out, will always be there to give us what we need at our deepest levels, and can in fact carry us though death and beyond, as if we were in fact mounted on some befriending, immortal dolphin.

But the truth is that we are all liable to be half-hearted about such a belief—likely to be volatile, edgy, sceptical, as indeed the first disciples were. What this really means is that we are adults in an adult world, where both demands and disappointments are many, where innocence is easily lost and cynicism is easily found. It is to just such people that the promises of Christ are made: it is for just such people that he died and rose: and it is with just such people in mind—ourselves, and those like us—that we are engaged in this Mass, where the whole muddled story of our distresses is told once more, and the promises of the Risen One are reiterated.

For much of life, we will be like the disciples fishing by night—with futility, as it seemed. The cockiness gets knocked out of us by various developments, and the danger is that its place will be taken by cynicism. Let us pray for one another, and for all of the Lord's hungry world, that we may at such moments remember that he is still on the shore, still calling to us, still kindling a fire, still putting together such food as we deeply need.

*Newman: April, 1995*

SILENCES

## *Earthquakes, et cetera*
### 19th Sunday in Ordinary Time, Year A

MELBOURNE IS NAMED AFTER LORD MELBOURNE, who taught the young Queen Victoria how to do the job: and Adelaide is named after Queen Adelaide, who is principally remembered as a name on wine bottles: and Darwin is named after Charles Darwin, who wrote *The Origin of Species*, and so changed the look of the world. When he was in his twenties, Darwin went on a scientific expedition which took years to complete, and which brought him round the globe, including a visit to Australia. In 1835 he went ashore at Concepcion, Chile, and saw the devastating effects of an earthquake—the collapse of buildings, the effects of fire, the looting. It was all very foreign: but he then imagined what it would be like if large-scale earthquakes broke out in England, with the inevitable commercial and social results. It would be the *end* of England in any recognizable sense.

Our first reading today lays on an earthquake, and a hurricane, and a fire. They are there for the benefit of the prophet Elijah. Nobody gets hurt in these, big though they are: they are a vivid, dramatic lesson, provided by God the Teacher. Elijah has been told in clear terms to go on alert before God, and, good man that he is, he is ready to do this. And then he is given such a show as he will never forget for the rest of his life—something mind-gripping, as Darwin's mind was gripped by the earthquake in Concepcion.

On the whole, we expect prophets in the Bible to be well-keyed to this kind of thing; they themselves are liable to talk fire-and-brimstone, upheavals and convulsions, and a great shortage of peace and quiet. It would not be surprising if our story culminated with the Lord showing himself in the fire—after all, he had done so to Moses in the Burning Bush: and the prophet Isaiah has any amount of blazing associated with divinity. But as we know, that is not how the story turns out. The Lord, this time, was not in the fire, nor in the hurricane, nor in the earthquake. It was the gentle breeze that made the difference to Elijah, as it was meant to. He covered his face, out of reverence, and waited for the Lord to speak.

What I hear in this story is a call for the stilling of the heart, a call for the patient eye, the patient ear: a call for the doing-almost-nothing of prayer. Mind, I am conscious of a certain irony in saying this, since they would give short odds on me in the Restlessness Stakes, and that is not much of a qualification, on the face of it, for praying well. It reminds me of what somebody said about the craggy, noisy nineteenth-century thinker Thomas Carlyle: that he praised silence in many volumes.

I am not alone in this predicament. And I take heart, and so may you, from the fact that before the gentle breeze there *were* the wind, and the earthquake, and the fire. We bring to prayer the persons we are, the things we have engaged in or undergone, and the seasons of our souls. But however we get there, and whatever we are like when we arrive, it is important that we do get there.

Cardinal Martini, the Archbishop of Milan, knows more than his prayers: he knows what it is like to deal with murderers, and with a degraded political system, and with a highly cynical constituency. He didn't learn all those languages he speaks just to say his prayers. But I was struck by a remark he made when talking about living ethically in the world of business. He said that the theory of business ethics is all very well, but if you truly want to be liberated from anger and fear, those great impediments to living well, you have to spend a significant amount of time in what is tantamount to prayer, or in actual prayer.

I live in a far milder milieu than that of much business life, milder I dare say than the milieu of many of you. But I have no doubt that what Martini says is true for me. How does it go for you?

*Newman: August, 1996*

VALETE

# Goodbye and Hello

ABOUT FIVE HUNDRED YEARS AGO, IN ENGLAND, people started saying 'goodbye' to each other. It's not that there had never been partings before, or that they took place soundlessly: but the word was a comparatively new one. It is in fact a collapsed version of 'God be with you': and I hope that, often, our word retains at least some trace of that older sense.

'God be with you' means at least two things. It means, 'May you live in a flourishing way, may unstaunched vitality be with you', and it means 'Since I cannot be with you, at least for a while, I entrust you to God'. Goodbyes are often occasions of sadness—as in the saying, and the song-title, 'Every time we say goodbye, I die a little'—but we hope that they may also be moments at which we can muster sweetness—can offer it, and receive it. To say goodbye to someone in a genuine way, not simply in a glancing or shrugging way, is to bless them. We pray them on their way, and we hope that our prayer for their good goes with them like a shadowy version of ourselves. To say goodbye to someone with all our heart is, in a sense, to stay with them after all.

Tonight might have been called 'Goodbye Night', and if it had been, it would have had some of the flavour I have just been describing. Certainly this Mass, which like all Masses is an offering of blessings all round, would then have such a flavour, and it still does.

Instead, we use a traditional Latin word, which comes into English simply as 'Fare-well'. 'Valete' means, 'as you fare (or go), may things go well for you'. The sense is much the same as in 'goodbye', but this time the stress is on health in the journey. To travel is not only to change place but to be exposed to changes in ourselves: our friends, and others who love us, care that in the midst of those changes we may gain more than we lose. 'Valete' is shorthand for all of that.

When you came to Newman, you had to say farewell to a past, and to places, and to people. In many cases, this was probably not too much of a wrench: novelty beckoned, your bodies and minds and hearts were blossoming, there was a world on offer. It was not necessarily like that for your parents, though, for whom your going may have been a little death, whatever jokes they made about it. But one way or another you have had some experience of the farewell business. And if your time at one university or another has been worthwhile, and if your time at Newman has been worthwhile, you will have had to do some more farewelling. One of the most famous books to be written about the experience of being a soldier in the first World War was called *Goodbye to All That*. Learning well involves saying goodbye to various biasses and prejudices, saying farewell to easy verbal and intellectual and emotional rides, saying so-long to cherished bits of pride and arrogance. Nobody ever learns deeply without being changed: deep learning is, in fact, itself a kind of change, and it requires us to leave behind a size of our selves which is now too small for us, as we have left behind clothes we have out-grown.

A Valete Mass, and a Valete Dinner, are ways of celebrating those out-growths, those farewells. Most of you are better than you were when you came here, and that is something for us all to celebrate. If you are indeed better, it is because, while saying goodbye to the outgrown, you have learned to say 'hello' to some new, some well-chosen, things. These include useful information, and novel insights, and encouraging policies, and some of what we call for short, 'wisdom'. You will have said hello to strategies of thought, even if they taxed you; and to challenging matters of fact, even if they vexed you; and to bodies of evidence, even if they sometimes exhausted you. You will, too, have grown in attention to the needs and excellences of people whom you did not always understand, and whom you might not even like, now or for the rest of your lives. Sometimes, as at this moment, you will have brought both your failures and your flair to the presence of the God who knows all our fragility and who blesses all our hopes. In so far as things like this have happened, it is appropriate indeed that we should be lighting candles to signal joy, listening to music to muster harmony, eating and drinking to bond ourselves as one Body, with one Spirit.

You will expect me to say, next, that things are not over yet, and so I do. The mingling of goodbye and hello, of fare-well and well-come, which I have just mentioned is the model for a whole life. The readings we have heard bear this out. St Paul's description of Christian love dwells on its dynamic elements—its vitality, its robustness, its tenacity. That love, he implies, is far from naive: it can weather storms, it can take rebuffs and not be daunted, it can sweat things out and still keep moving. To love maturely requires that we say goodbye, again and again, to illusions—whether about ourselves or about others—without resorting to mere cynicism. And it requires that we welcome new opportunities to give of our best for the world's sake, even though, as Paul says, 'our knowledge is imperfect and our prophesying is imperfect'—even though we can never entirely command any human situation, and have to try to keep loving in shadowed circumstances and to some extent across the grain of our own wariness. 'When I became a man I put childish ways aside', the apostle says: but the putting aside of infantile behaviour for the sake of needed love is not a thing easily done with in this life.

Our Gospel passage, too, reminds us of the need to go on welcoming the tasks of love. Mary Magdalene, driven by love even while numbed with grief, is intent on doing one final service for the dead Christ. She is forced to become a searcher—the last thing she must have wanted in the circumstances. She greets the man whom she takes for the gardener, and is greeted in turn in a way which transforms her understanding, and transfigures her hopes. And then she is charged with a further task, for the sake of those who have always been within the ambit of Christ's love—which means, in effect, all human beings who have ever lived.

'Goodbyes are often occasions of sadness—
as in the saying, and the song-title,
"Every time we say goodbye, I die a little"—
but we hope that they may also be moments
at which we can muster sweetness—
can offer it, and receive it.'

Here, too, in this dramatic episode, we can see that all that has been most precious in our past must be reconfigured in memory and in hope: that our desiring hearts must work together with our designing minds, so that we may flourish, by God's grace, and flourish in the only thoroughly worthwhile way, which is in the service of others. The others will often not look as though they are worth it: but then, on the evidence of the gospels, the apostles themselves, Jesus' companions, often did not look as though they were worth it; but they needed it, and so they got it. What they also got was several years of schooling in the ways of love and the path of joy. Let us pray for one another, this evening, that it may always be so with us.

*Newman: November, 1998*

# PEOPLE

DINNY
O'HEARN

# Hospitality of the Heart

DINNY MADE AS LIGHT AS HE COULD OF OUR being caught in the toils of mortality, but even he would grant that this is a bitter day for us all. Bitterest of all for his fiancee Kim, to whom our hearts go out at this moment. Until last week, the plan was that they were to have been married, yesterday, in this College. There is a cruel irony in our gathering instead, as we now do, to celebrate this dear man, but also to farewell him.

Even those who knew and loved him through most of his life will grant readily enough that none of us knew him in all his variety: if you were for some reason a Dinny-watcher, there was always more to see. So I do not pretend, in a few minutes, to name all that was treasurable about him. His faults were few, and are none of my business here. Each of you, probably, will remember the good things that made him so splendidly himself. Some of these will be mentioned near the end of this service, and all of them will be recalled elsewhere. Just now, as is the tradition of the Christian churches, I want to unfold from the scriptural readings we have just heard something relevant to Dinny.

I chose from the gospels the passage naming various forms of human blessedness—the 'Beatitudes'. The Christ who named and commended them had a warrant for doing so—the warrant of his own character and lived experience. To reflect on them is to find his lineaments becoming clearer. But it is also to find the all-important human dynamic—a love of, and a commitment to, life itself. The ultimately sacred thing is life, be it divine or human or both; the ultimately treasurable thing is life, be it divine or human or both. Some people have the gift to feel that in their bones, and the energy of spirit to live accordingly. Dinny was one of them. In all sobriety, you could, in his company, be filled with vivacity—and of course it didn't have to be all sobriety. His great intelligence and his great, informal learning, could be deployed in a variety of ways, but the object of the exercise was always very largely to make one's own personal world ampler, more habitable, and more companionable. There's an Australian comedy routine in which the actor says, 'We all like life, don't we—it's something to do'. For Dinny, life wasn't something to do, but the great thing to be drawn from, added to, and above all shared.

This could take the well-known and much-remarked on forms: if conviviality had not been invented, Dinny was just the man to do the job. But it could also take the form of patient preparation, of legwork and hackwork, of institutional panache and finesse in the midst of recurring scepticism about the institutional. And it could take the form of loyal, compassionate, shrewd and wise counsel and companionship. Universities can be great nurseries of pettiness—of vanity and domineering and facile cruelty. Dinny, who had no illusions about all this pathetic nonsense, outflanked a lot of it by dexterity in manoeuvre, but outfaced a lot more by the calibre of his own generous personality. And what was at stake almost always was the opportunity for students or staff to flourish. He knew that being a participant in life is all very well, but that being one of life's partisans was better still. The teaching he did in classrooms, dashing though that could be, was the least important of his teaching.

The other major scriptural reading today, from St Paul's letter to the Christians in Rome, is frank about the fact that taking heart and fostering creativity have often to be done against the grain of experience. His claim was that, in the person of Christ, God continues to invest himself in our death-prone world, to bring it a love which will one day conquer even death. Dinny, certainly, and to the end, was on the side of taking heart and on the side of creativity. My last image of him is the wink and the thumbs-up which he gave me as I left, hours before he died. It was of a piece with all the geniality and vivacity which he had showed so long and so famously: but it rose out of horrible humiliation and suffering. His was a contending spirit, in a good cause.

Even when things were less drastic, he tackled things. He fostered Australian writing, not as an abstraction, but as part of the address which we all make to one another. The Book Show, in which he made a last interview two weeks ago, always tried to be both intellectual and companionable. Even the forays to Ireland which he relished so much were also exercises in the interpretation of one people to another. A glance around this chapel today will show an uncommonly large span of people, diverse in tastes and talents, most of whom were Dinny's friends. You do not span so many unless you do some reaching. Dinny's hospitality of heart may have been an instinctive thing, but it was also a taxing thing. He loved us, but it did not always come easily.

Time presses, and I conclude by saying three things. The first is to reiterate our sympathies to all who were nearest to him, and all who loved him most. The second is to thank his doctors, and the nursing staff, especially, of Peter MacCallum Hospital, who helped him in his illness, and all the hundreds of people who offered their concern and compassion at that time. The third is to affirm the faith of the Church that Dinny is and will remain more than a memory—that the Christ who died and rose for him will raise him up from death. Not all of us here today share that faith. What we do share is gratitude for Dinny's life among us, and grief at his going. The world is the worse for his absence, and we are the better for having known his presence.

*July, 1993*

NOEL
RYAN SJ

## *An Original*

WHEN MANY OF US WHO ARE HERE TODAY MET in this chapel last year to farewell Noel Ryan's old friend Ted Stormon, the ceremony included a reading from Dante's *Divine Comedy*. Something similar would be appropriate for Noel, since he had a pronounced sense that life is comic. Psychologists speak of free-floating emotion: Noel had a free-floating smile, ready for application to whatever instance of the ludicrous might happen to present itself next. But behind the smile, and giving it some of its warrant, was a strong sense that everything was after all in God's hands, and that we should proceed resolutely.

Noel was to a high degree a 'hearer of the word', whether in its secular or in its sacred forms, and it is more than usually appropriate that we should, on his behalf and in his company, listen once again to what the Lord says to us in today's readings. In his letter to the converts in Rome, Paul gives us variations on the theme of Christian liberty. 'The spirit you received is not the spirit of slaves bringing fear into your lives again; it is the spirit of sons, and it makes us cry out, "Abba, Father!"' Noel was par excellence an intellectual, and such people are prone to the intimidations that come from looking into the labyrinth of life. He was not exempt from the daytime equivalents of nightsweats and nightmares. But what kept him at his apostolic pursuits was not only a native tenacity of purpose, but also an unassuming faith. A labyrinth can turn anyone into a child, and an intimidated child at that; but there was an essential simplicity about Noel which could be expressed aptly in the cry, 'Abba, Father'. Kierkegaard said that 'purity of heart is to will one thing'; Noel had that purity of heart, and he knew very well that it was not his own doing.

But Christian liberation is concerned not only with a personal enhancement, but with the sponsoring of freedom in others. On the memorial card for Noel there is printed a passage from the teachings of the Second Vatican Council, which is a reminder of the privilege and the onus of fraternal liberation. In the later years of his life, Noel was tireless in his activities on behalf of religious liberty—not the most popular of causes in Australia. I know that there are people here today who are grateful to him for that. Those of us who knew him in earlier years should not be surprised at this engagement of his, since the thrust of much of his teaching at that time, whether it was literary or philosophical or pedagogical or sociological, was towards the opening of new vistas and the nerving of his hearers to think in new ways. One might be disconcerted, momentarily, by the motorbike saddlebag-full of recommended books, or by the bibliographies which begat bibliographies: but where all this was going was in the direction of ampler understanding and more generous relishment. There was also his ironical disposition towards overweening authority. He said of one of his Jesuit superiors, 'Father Rector behaves like a Gestapo agent until the last moment, and then turns into a gentleman'. And, alluding to more momentous forces, 'It's good that you are a poet: over in Rome, they think that all poets are mad, and they leave them alone'. Beyond these Wodehousean frivolities—and he did love Wodehouse—there was his instinctive sense of liberty's moral grandeur. A follower of George Washington said that 'freedom is a light for which many men have died in the darkness'. Noel knew what that was all about, but he worked on behalf of many men's, and many women's, enjoying the light.

St Paul, in the same passage, speaks of the entire creation's 'groaning in one great act of giving birth', and he says that 'we too groan inwardly as we wait to be set free'. This is what might fairly be called 'the big picture', and Noel was always one for that: you don't voluntarily mess with Hegel, for instance, unless large schemata are on your mind. Mere largeness may be lunacy, of course, reverberant with vacuity: but that is not the Pauline way, and it was not Noel's. He thought of the Church at large, and of the world at large, and he thought for both of them: but he never supposed that our collective liberation from sin, folly and death would be an easy ride. What St Paul calls creation's 'slavery to decadence' was something against which Noel could cry out, comically or, as he used to say, in 'deadly serious' vein. Still, he had a lyricist's heart, not a satirist's: he knew that the Lord of the *Commedia* would have the last word.

That Lord is displayed to us, in Jesus his Icon, in the passage we have heard from Luke's Gospel. There, the disciples say to the unrecognized Jesus, 'Our own hope had been that he would be the one to set Israel free'. Thereupon, they are met by a reminder that there are, so to speak, no ring-roads around life's density: that the City of Man has to be dwelt in if the City of God is to come to expression; that the providential past has to be consulted and consented to if a luminous future is to have any viability. This being ready to garner human experience, to appraise it, and learn from it, and extend it, has also been an important mark of Christian humanism, whether at the hands of the Church Fathers—and Mothers, as we are learning to see—or of people like More and Erasmus, or of various assayers of God in the flesh of the late twentieth century. Noel was all for the discerning of grace even in partly disgraced or disgraceful contexts: and while he could be memorably frank about human idiocy and perversity, he was essentially a celebrant of human possibility when it is infused with divine vitality. As a priest, for forty-three and a half years 'he took the bread and said the blessing; then he broke it and handed it to them'. Doing this in our present ritual, he was keeping faith both with a divine commissioning and with human needs. I am not the only one whose heart has burned within him when Noel talked to us on the road and articulated the divine sayings and the divine deeds.

All of us have our memories of him: and none is more authoritative than another. Paul Goodman said of the moon-shots, much criticized for their expense, but also much admired, 'People will find value where they will find value', and that was Noel's attitude. He loped and stalked and occasionally ricochetted through life as God's treasure-hunter and treasure-endorser. Anybody could see that he was clever, and he had knowledge the way most of us have ignorance: but the wisdom was far more important than the knowledge, and you do not get that from reading books. He was a workaholic, of course, but he could almost give a good name to that perilous condition. And, conspicuously, he was an original—a good idea that did not go wrong, and is unlikely to be replicated.

We say of those we have loved that they will be missed, and we would be the slighter if we did not think this. Some of us, young and old, will miss Noel, though most of us believe that this will be only for a while. Many years ago, improbably enough, he introduced me to Rabelais. This morning, I remember that one version of Rabelais' last words is, 'Ring down the curtain: the comedy is finished'. But for Noel—and he is just the person to enjoy it—the real comedy has just begun.

6 September, 1993

SEAMUS
HEANEY

# *Past Master*

I KNOW A FEW PEOPLE WHO ARE INTENT ON THE demolition of the past, and their principal visible attribute is a compound of self-fear and self-hatred. I doubt whether this is an accident. Seamus Heaney calls the sense of the past 'a fundamental human gift, as potentially civilizing as our gift for love'; and although gifts may, as the Trojans found, be tainted, they are not so in principle, and in fact their bent is to tell against taint. As things go when we are in good cultural health, a sense of the past is a cherishable thing. As Heaney also says of certain dear, laden entities, 'The air which our imaginations inhale in their presence is not musty but bracing'.

This has nothing to do with a sentimentalizing of the past. The dictionaries of quotations regularly report Gibbonian jeers at the past's configuration. What adult, what adolescent, what half-way alert child, cannot cite murk and shadow from the past? We are all our own messengers of bad news from the country left behind. But such tidings say nothing about the wholeness of the tale.

I cannot think of a single substantial intellectual movement in, say, the last two hundred years, which has not had at the centre of its concern the matter of what we are to do about the past. The truly bestial policy is that adopted briefly in Cambodia, where memory and chronicle were, as far as possible, washed away in blood. Less extreme versions of this have had their currency on the left and on the right. At the opposite extreme, less savage but incited by potent fears, there have been all the recoilings from novelty as if it were the maw of disaster—all the movements commending 'back to' this or that, as though the past were not deathly in its own ways, and as though our present ills had not been bred precisely by the past. So there is an abundance of ways to blunder in our confronting the past, and there is no magically efficacious directive to avert any particular blunder.

But there really is nowhere else to go: the only avenue to the future invariably spirals through the past. Dante, in his genius, constructs the whole of the *Divine Comedy* around just such a spiral: the past is, hundreds of times, re-encompassed as the path to the amplest of futures. It is not antiquarianism to notice this: Mandelshtam, that most unbridled of modern poets, conceived of his project as a dialogue with Dante. On a different plane, Freud, whose distaste for religion was unconditional, and who thought his task to be one of opening the eyes of the blind in order to aid them to face a bleak enough future, always took it that the backward gaze was a prerequisite for wisdom. And such history of science as I know always suggests that it is the models of reality offered by the past which, inverted, reappropriated, or expanded, generate the new interpretations. We see in the faces of our parents the foreshadowed faces of our children.

Still, the mediators, the interveners, are ourselves, and we know this. Automata could not conceive even the notion of automata, let alone of variety. Heaney is right—there is a bracing air to be inhaled, and we are the inhalers, the in-haulers. One way of looking at Christ is to see him as a person braced by the inhalation of the past, as a 'past master' in that sense. He wanted to be its beneficiary, not its pawn. He appealed much to its authority, co-reading his people's reading of events. He went so far as to read himself into the existing scriptures: his affront to the Scribes was that he inscribed himself into the text, which none of them, sensibly, had ever done. He sacralized his own transient self by unprecedented appeal to the 'perpetualized', and thus godly, word.

And at the same time he offered himself as the ultimate revisionist, the final redactor of formulations, the re-steeper in time of tales long secured. Any fool of a wrecker can do this, and foolish wreckers do it to this day. The critically important thing is not whether someone offers, as Marvell said of Cromwell, 'to ruin the great work of time', but whether the yield from such a venture looks like having warranted the fierce intervention.

It seems to me that one cannot find the answer to that question simply as a spectator. The person who knows whether the revolution was worthwhile is not, on the whole, the historian, but the revolutionary, and whoever stood on the other side, and whoever fell between them. Shaw said, cynically but usefully, 'there was only one Christian, and he died on a cross': usefully, because, as claimers of the name of Christians have always attested, they too have to take the cross, so long as that is above all the insignia of their keeping faith with others in their need. To 'take the cross' for any other reason, one might as well be an aztec, or a nazi.

'As potentially civilizing as our gift for love', Heaney said. To be civilized is above all to be schooled in conviviality, that movement which puts the midwife's hand around the emerging child, and the nurse's hand to the cheek of the dying man. In the hundreds of thousands of gestures in between these which we have all known, what we have been looking for, in spite of our fears and hatreds, has been the tidal movement of love. Neither Jesus, nor any religion, is of the slightest worth, unless they serve that purpose. If they have a claim on us, it is because they do.

*Anglesea: 26 February, 1993*

JIM
HACKER

# *Not the Prime Minister*

### 31st Sunday in Ordinary Time, Year A

IF YOU NEVER SAW ANY OF THE TELEVISION episodes of 'Yes, Minister' or 'Yes, Prime Minister,' do not be disappointed. Surely they will be back, as they have already been, once or twice. If you did see them, you will remember one trait of their 'hero,' Jim Hacker—namely, his readiness to identify himself with his official role, his proneness to all-but-lose himself in that role. He was in fact, as every episode in the series made clear, a political mediocrity; but from time to time, with a little judicious prompting, he would brace himself, stare into the middle distance, and adopt the phrases and verbal mannerisms of Winston Churchill. He would sound, momentarily, like the reincarnation of that celebrated statesman.

Pretty smartly, somebody would cut his perch out from under him. His Head of Department would do it with an awkward question; his wife would do it with a laugh. And there the poor fellow would be, down to earth with the rest of us, his role and its rhetoric dangling up in the clouds, while he had once more to get on with living life as it truly is. I suspect that one reason for the popularity of this series was that Jim Hacker was instantly recognizable as a type; and not just a political type. Hordes of people, given a bit of promotion, a bit of elevation, get carried away with it all, and play such ridiculous parts, as Shakespeare once said, as 'make the angels weep,' though he did not say whether the weeping came from grief and frustration or from laughter.

'... the ass and the harp together remind me
that God both declines to take pretension
seriously and draws beautiful music out
of simple creatures.'

*People*

It makes a good show, then, and may there be many more of the same kind. But it also resonates with what our Lord says to us in today's Gospel. In that, he speaks acidly of pompous and hypocritical performance; he scorns the confusion of action with swaggering around, and he says so. And in fact, after the twelve verses which make up the Gospel today, he cuts loose with another twenty-seven verses which get more and more bitter. If he said this sort of thing in Australia today, about certain people, he would find a writ slapped on him; as it was, nobody sued him, but the powerful criticized people had stark memories, and they helped to bring him to a disgusting death.

I don't want to be easily theatrical about these matters; and after all, nobody in this chapel is likely to go to bed tonight winceing with distaste for the Scribes or the Pharisees, any more than we do at the Pharaohs or the ancient Emperors of China. But there are still lessons to be had, for all of us, from this Gospel. And one of them, as I take it, is that we do well to come to God without roles. Jesus says to us, in this passage, 'Whoever lifts himself up will be tumbled down, but whoever does not lift himself up will be gathered up after all.' The most important way of not-being-lifted-up is in the declining to have a role before God—the being, nakedly, the self God has made me, whoever on earth that is. Without style, without much shape, in the dumpy, staggering, blundering fashion of a baby, I may find at last what it is to know God as the mothering, fathering person who gave me birth, and can give me re-birth.

On one of the exterior walls of Chartres Cathedral, there is a stone ass playing a stone harp. They have been there for hundreds of years, through war and peace in France, through the lives and deaths of kings, and the French Revolution, and all of Napoleon's monomaniacal carry-on, and many philosophical and political and artistic and theological and social movements. Perhaps they will be there for, say, another thousand years: I hope so. And I hope so because the ass and the harp together remind me that God both declines to take pretension seriously and draws beautiful music out of simple creatures.

Here I am, at this moment, decked out with ceremonial garb,

and playing the little harp of this homily. I would be a great fool to suppose that my present role was the complete truth about me, and certainly none of you is so foolish as to suppose that; in the end, I am, as you are, naked before our loving Lord at this moment, naked before the maker of asses and harps. When we leave this chapel, may God grant us to move with some serenity, and some freedom, as people who simply entrust themselves to him. Jesus, like the rest of us, came naked into the world; and like the rest of us, he went, in effect, naked out of it. In between, he kept on offering himself, simply, to the good God, as frankly as an ass. As a direct result, it is by the splendid music of his resurrection that we make such loving moves as we can manage, today.

*Newman: 1996*

WILLIAM
SHAKESPEARE

# *Shifts of the Spirit*

THESE DAYS, METAMORPHOSIS IS ON MY MIND. I have been teaching a course lately about travel writing, and now I am trying to deal with change in Shakespeare. And since I like cooking and cookbooks, and since cookery is all transformation, the old Ovidian and Parmenidean preoccupations crop up.

Travel, Shakespeare, or cooking—there is good news and bad news in them. A farcical or tragical library could be assembled of books which deal with all that can go wrong in, and from, travel. All the deplorers of the Colombian centenary wish that Columbus had stayed home; so, from time to time, must he have done, when things went sour. While his or any other travel was taking place, stresses would be normal, adjustments constant, life taxing. At the same time, the animating hope of the trip in the first place is that it will make for relief, vindication, instruction—anyway, betterment. Good news, bad news—they intertwine like the snakes on a caduceus, or the elements in the double helix.

It is the same story with Shakespeare, as, increasingly, he himself acknowledges. When he speaks of sweet sorrow, or of the heart, between 'two extremes of joy and grief', that 'burst smilingly', this is partly the renaissance paradox game, but it is more deeply the expression of his sense that one condition melts into another, melds with another. Depending on the perspective offered by time, psyche, and circumstance, much will be identified as good or as bad news. Either way, the labile condition of humanity, as represented in the little band which he assembles to play the story out in any individual drama, itself goes on being explored in mutable ways. In spite of the encomia of the ages, Shakespeare did not do this in ways satisfactory to all. Voltaire thought him a barbarian. In the eighteenth century his plays were rewritten. In the twentieth century he has sometimes been found not so much compendious as manipulative. Change is his topic, his element, and his fate.

Cookery is all change. Boil an egg, and you change an expectation, as well as the egg. It is a disconcerting and perhaps a haunting thing to think of the thousands of millions of times that utterly forgotten people have engaged in this process of transmutation—everything from singeing a wodge of blood-dripping meat to bringing off the alchemy of the master-chef. We all know, to our cost, what can go wrong. Someone said of a particular meal to which he had been invited, 'the wine was a comedy and the food was a tragedy': we see what he meant. Things go deeper than social fiasco, in the land of food. Uninstructed or desperate measures lead to malnutrition, poisoning, death. And on the other hand, the amount of festive, heartened, and exhilarated life that has been sponsored by well-made meals, with food and drink, is impossible to calculate.

Travel is for the soul and the body; so is Shakespeare; so is making meals together. All of them are circumstances of the Spirit. Generations of youngsters learned, once, about the missionary journeys of St Paul—events full of the palpable, the meaningful, and the momentous. Pilgrimage re-enacted more important journeys than Paul's, namely those of Jesus, and above all his being and going a 'Way' which was offered as the paradigm for all apt human procedure. Secular travel too is darted through with senses for the soul as well as senses for the body. A Sunday drive, a Monday commuter ride—either way, we are participants in meaning, with its zebra-like coat.

Shakespeare is for soul and body. For the eye, and the mouth, and the actorly body: for the ensemble of those who put themselves close to the events on the stage, and become a kind of body-in-one

'Travel, Shakespeare, or cooking—there is
good news and bad news in them. A farcical
or tragical library could be assembled of
books which deal with all that can go wrong
in, and from, travel.'

themselves. Also for the soul, which is always in search of fleshed-out meaning, the true as distinct from the nightmarish countenance of menace, the face of hope and joy. We put ourselves to school with Shakespeare, not to learn about him, but to learn about ourselves. And the more we do this, the more we find that aspiration and enactment, gambit and counter-gambit, are the staples of our being.

All of us gaze out of the turret of our bodies through the lenses of our eyes. We never, directly, see ourselves, straight. The mirror turns us around, every time. The photograph shows us flat, every time. The video shows us 'as filmed', every time. So it goes with heart, with soul. But when, in the mode of drama, we find body and soul being played out for our observation, a self-recognizing figure within us stands up and says, 'present!'. In Shakespeare, none of this, for all his affection for the universal aphorism, takes place except in the modality of change. He is the Merlin of the mind, both in the magician's command and in his vulnerability.

And the Spirit? The Spirit is, by definition, shift. The Spirit is Change-for-the-Better. In our ordinary use of the language, we often have doubts about shift. 'Shifty' is never good news; 'making shift' is a second-best; 'shifting' is a saying on which the jury is still out. These are all metamorphoses, and we have a wary eye on them. We have a wary eye on the Spirit, too. Ignatius' injunction that we should be discerning about authentic and bogus 'spirits' is licensed by Paul, and implicitly by Jesus. It is also a matter of common sense. That the diabolical apes the divine does not need scriptural or theological warrant: it is a feature of the experience of every adult. But after all that is allowed, the Spirit bids for change. Lichtenberg says, 'powerful imaginations are conservative', and the powerful imagination of the Spirit conserves, all right—retrieves, refreshes, re-embraces—but always imaginatively, always going up and up in scope.

I do not say these things out of temperamental disposition, much less moral zest. If I had a coat of arms, everything on it would be couchant, except for a Giant Sloth, rampant. Were I a Beatle, the song would have been, 'All we are saying is/ Leave things alone'. Unfortunately, as also happened to Ignatius, the wind has changed, and the Spirit has got into my craw. The thing that keeps the world un-converted, un-transfigured, is not resistance to this or that specific change, but fear and revulsion at change itself. The iced-up heart is the berg on which all creativity founders.

I have quoted before, and it will bear quoting again, the conclusion of Rilke's 'Archaic Torso of Apollo'. In this poem, the poet, gazing at the brilliant beauty of the statue, says finally, 'for here there is no place/ that does not see you. You must change your life'. It is an astonishing conclusion. *'You must change your life'* is enjoined not by some moralizing intransigent, but by a relisher addressing the relishable. This is what Ignatius, also, was up to. It was not the sullen cowl of distaste for the world, but the lucky caul of hope for it, that made him so eager that things not be allowed to stay as they stood. When Jesuits and others, invoking the Ignatian tradition, have been content to stand pat with the status quo, they have in fact been like the many who have wanted the Archaic Torso to be buried, rather than reared, in a museum. But a museum is not a mausoleum. It is a place where the Muses muse, a hive for honeycomb. The keepers of tradition should be not the gaolers but the stagers of the Spirit, the fosterers of all that makes for hope.

We wake, every day, to the same old world, the same old tale. As did Jesus. Even the most novel of territories is immensely older than its inhabitants; even the most newly-cast of societies is institutionalized into quasi-inevitability in days, let alone centuries. Someone said that 'everyone complains about the weather, but nobody *does* anything about it': everybody says that you can't beat City Hall. Years ago I found a card that said, 'When in doubt, panic'; another said, 'If at first you don't succeed, quit'. I take the points, I get the jokes. But contrary to what is often suggested, these are not the nervously-framed fruits of deeply-versed lives. They are prattlement. They are the sayings of those who have signed-off before adulthood. Out there, in here, in their despite, there is a sleeping Spirit, waiting for nothing more than to be awakened by the kiss of yearning.

*Newman: July, 1992*

# PLACES

COMMUNITY

# *Grass, Squirrel, Christ*
Wednesday, Week 4, Year I

IF YOU COME TO THESE UNITED STATES FROM Australia, you will have seen plenty of kangaroos, but you probably won't have seen a squirrel, so you'll notice them. I know that the squirrels keep their heads down a bit during winter, but when things warm up they will be on the move again, and hardly anyone will spare them a second glance. In both countries, there is plenty of grass: here, it is pretty scruffy when snow threatens, and there, it doesn't have much of a time when the temperature is at about 105 degrees: but it is quite commonplace—the Psalmist, and Jesus himself, speak of grass as the finally casual thing.

Grass and squirrels are ordinary flora, ordinary fauna, and have been so for uncounted millions of people. But this is what the nineteenth-century novelist George Eliot wrote, in words which continue to grip readers:

> 'If we had a keen vision and feeling of all ordinary human life, it would be like hearing the grass grow and the squirrel's heart beat, and we should die of that roar which lies on the other side of silence.'

'Like hearing the grass grow and the squirrel's heart beat.' The point here is that Eliot is intent on what she calls 'all ordinary human life'. She does not choose as her examples some titanic tree or some thunderous being like the whale: she takes the sort of thing that has been there for the observing outside of this building and millions of other buildings. She was, on the whole, a genius of the ordinary: her heroes or heroines might be singular, but she applauded above all their having a singular keenness of attention to the way things go from moment to moment, from day to day. It was a sorrow to George Eliot, as to others of her generation, that they could not believe, or could no longer believe, in a God of all this. But, as both of our readings in the Eucharist remind us today, we are called to hold that belief, and to live by it.

The writer of the Letter to the Hebrews has been trying to brace his readers and hearers with the memory of those gone before them. Some of these are named in heroic terms—the muzzlers of lions, the dousers of fire, the routers of armies. Some of them are people who are no such stellar performers—they were, says the writer, 'in poverty, distress and misery'. When he comes to today's passage, we are challenged to stiffen our drooping arms and shaking knees, and to keep our steps from wavering. Unless you have had a particularly good day today, and have a short memory, you will recognize what he is talking about. Our lives are ordinary lives: we are ordinary people. However many photographs they may take of us, however often our names are bandied about, we look in the mirror and we see the truth.

We are as ordinary as squirrels, as ordinary as grass. And yet, isn't it true that all our education as Christians, and certainly all our education as people of the Ignatian ethos, forbids us to take that as the whole story? Ignatius the mystic could have spoken to George Eliot, and she would have known what he was talking about, for he too was riveted, was magnetized, by a sense of the astounding, the divine, in the thick of the ordinary. Every significant moment in the *Spiritual Exercises*, from the *First Principle and Foundation* to the *Contemplation for Obtaining Love*, brings to a needle-sharp point the intimate relationship between ordinariness and the extraordinary, a relationship in which we may say that the one becomes the other—and in both directions: the ordinary becomes the extraordinary, the extraordinary the ordinary. The world's flesh is of the Word's making.

*Places*

Ignatius was convinced of this, and he was so not because he had had some esoteric philosophical or mystagogical insight, but because the fact of the fleshed God had come home to him. We all know the story of his doing in effect what the editors of some twentieth-century Bibles have done—putting the words of the Lord in red. But our Lord was not Confucius, or an eighteenth-century aphorist; and his vivid words matter only insofar as they are braided or plaited in with the story of his living the common days, his engaging with common people, who walked on grass among small animals. When Ignatius appeals in the Exercises, and in different style but with no less force in the Constitutions, that we go on putting ourselves in Christ's company and be of Christ's Company, he does this as someone convinced that each of us is of one flesh with God made flesh, and that our common days are indeed irradiated with the true, or real, presence of Christ.

Now this, although we have all heard it a thousand times, is start-ling stuff. If we did indeed, as George Eliot almost said, have a keen vision and feeling of *this* all the time, we might die of that roar which lies on the other side of silence. But we don't, and at one level just as well too: none of us would be able to drive a car without collision, or, come to that, find our way out of this chapel; and neither Father Provincial nor Father General, spiritual men though they are, would be pleased by that. God tempers the wind to the shorn lambs, and we will find our ways to bed tonight.

But not I hope without taking the force of our Lord's challenge to us in our Gospel passage. There, you remember, the congregation in the hometown synagogue on the one hand acknowledges that Jesus is teaching with amazing force and wisdom and is working wonders: and on the other hand scales all this back with the reflection that he is a local boy, that they know his (presumably unremarkable) relations, and need they say more?

Mark's Gospel tells us that Jesus was taken aback by their want of faith—not the last time, by any means, that this will happen to him. He didn't want applause from them—he wasn't P. T. Barnum—he wanted insight from them, and that spin to the helm or twist of the steering-wheel that insight can bring. And in all honesty, don't we have to say that this is what he wants from us, tonight, and on the other nights and days—a shaking-up of the gestalt in which we usually see many things, and a settling into our hearts of a revised sense of priorities? Ignatius conjured us to try to find God in all things; the poet David Craig, in a poem called 'Pentecost,' asks *in toto*, 'What is this Holy Spirit?/ And what is it doing in the eggplant?' You can substitute a different word for 'eggplant' according to taste, but the question is still the one to ask. Divination is the name of our game.

This will not, for most of us, take us clear of many of our present circumstances or tasks: we are called to stay among the squirrels and grass, and all the things for which they might be emblems—the classrooms and computers and casual conversations. But I suppose that that Lord, our current Lord, wants to move us on from spiritual agnosia. Medical agnosia is that condition in which things don't hang together significantly; if you had agnosia, and I brought you out the front here and turned you to face the others, you mightn't know who or what they were. The dear Lord, in his Spirit, may be asking each of us, through tonight's readings, how far agnosia has advanced in us. Fortunately, at his hands, the condition is not incurable.

*Georgetown: February, 1997*

MARRIAGE

## *Friends Marrying*

NO DOUBT THE WORDS WE ALL WANT TO HEAR this evening are the 'I do' which are to be spoken by our two friends, in a few minutes' time. But they have chosen to say these in the context of those readings from God's word to which we have just listened; so for their sake, and for yours, I want to break open the bread of that word and show a little of what is inside it.

What I have to say can be summarized by claiming that the readings name a triple bonding: a bonding between the generations, a bonding between individuals, and a bonding between God's life and ours.

When, in the first brief passage, Ruth says, 'wherever you go, I will go: wherever you live, I will live. Your people shall be my people, and your God, my God', she is not speaking to her husband, who is in fact dead: she is speaking to her mother-in-law. This of course has a poignancy, which any of us could identify: but it also has a preciousness. It is precious because it marks an achievement which any developed community hopes for, but which can never be guaranteed—I mean, the passing on of affectionate understanding, of love indeed, from one generation to another.

We have all heard plenty about generation gaps, but if one of these did set in completely that would be the end of civilization, and perhaps of us all. It would mean that the young despaired of the past, the old despaired of the future: very soon, we as a race would have neither a past nor a future. This sorry state of affairs is fended off not mainly by argument, but by bondings in love between one generation and another. The love is often perplexed: the love, like most loves, comes to be wounded sooner or later: but it is also the love that makes the world go round. Young or old, all of us here this evening are witnesses to the folding of new loves into older ones—and of the promise of loves yet to be. That is something for which to thank God, as we do: it is also something for which to thank Georgina and Sam.

And then there is the reading from St Paul to his convert Christians in Corinth, of which I would say that it celebrates our being bonded with one another as individuals. Corinth was not an elegant or gentle place: it was a sea-port overlooked by a hill best-known for its association with ritual prostitution. Plenty of people lived hard, fast, and cruelly when they were there. So again there is a poignancy in Paul's commending to his converts not just a fair go for other people, not just a civilized tolerance, but a delicacy of attention, a finesse of concern, a loving wish to bring out the very best that could be found in one another.

'Love', says Paul, 'does not come to an end.' What a claim! What a lot to swallow! We have all seen individual relationships founder, seen them go down in the quicksands of anger, grief, resentment; less dramatically, we have seen them—perhaps in ourselves— dry up and blow away like so much chaff. And, God knows, the mid-day news and the evening news and the late-night news report the evaporation of affection between this group and that. In the face of all this experience, cynicism is seductive. We can become so accustomed to writing people off that we scarcely know that we are doing it.

Against all that, what Georgie and Sam are doing tonight is a retort: as a poet I like says, they are going to smile and spit into the face of death. And when they do, they will be the inheritors of what has been done not only by the likes of Ruth but by the likes of many good women and men in our own century. Often, since I read it, I have thought, for instance, of Count Helmuth von Moltke, a German general who was executed for his part in a plot to kill Hitler. He wrote to his wife on the evening of his execution to say that she had been his thirteenth chapter of the letter to the Corinthians—our chapter tonight: that she in her thoroughly-known body and spirit had been the word of God to him. It was the best compliment he could possibly pay her, especially in the circumstances. In our own entirely joyous circumstances, what we can hope for tonight is that Georgie and Sam will disclose to each other paths of love which nobody has every shown to anyone else before. It is neither rash nor sentimental to hope and pray for this: it is simply one of the things for which each of them was created.

All of this fringes on what is proclaimed to us in our Gospel passage, in which Jesus plaits together the language of our love for one another, the language of his love for us and ours for him, and the language of love between our whole array and the mysterious Father who originates everything and is the destination of everything. Probably the artistic work which, so far, has best represented all this is Dante's *Divine Comedy*; and people who know nothing else about that astounding work know that it ends with a reference to 'the Love that moves the sun and the other stars'. The 'Love' in question there is God himself, the God who is, if I may put it like this, a Divine Idiot who can't learn anything except loving, who is an indeflectible lover. That is the one to whom Jesus is referring in John's Gospel. The point of having a wedding service lodged in the midst of a Mass, a Eucharist, is that this is a way of claiming the concern of the Indeflectible Lover.

For the Mass always talks about the better and the worse, the sickness and the health, the good times and the bad—the *very* bad ones, and the *very* good ones. The Dante who rhapsodized about the Love that moves the sun and the other stars wrote in exile, and under sentence of death from Florence, his native, exiling city. That is to say, he wrote with about as few illusions as it is possible for a human being to have. Tonight, gifted with whatever personal loves we enjoy, we join gratefully to witness Georgie's and Sam's doing something of and for themselves, but also something of and for us all. We see and hear them at the heart of something which is much ampler than the 'world-wide-web' of recent technology. We see and hear them at the heart of a cosmic and eternal web of creativity, of lucidity, and of love. They honour us by having us here. Let us honour them with our prayers.

*for Georgina and Sam, September, 1996*

AMERICA

# *Home*
### Thanksgiving Day

IT HAS BEEN SAID THAT IN NO LANGUAGE ARE THE overtones of the word 'home' just what they are in English. Certainly, in America, that word has a special aura about it. 'Home for Thanksgiving,' 'home free,' 'home before dark,' 'homey': all of them imply excellence and welcome. When Robert Frost wrote, 'Home is the place where, when you have to go there, / They have to take you in', he spoke for many millions of us. The very claim on 'life, liberty and the pursuit of happiness' is a claim on being at home in the world.

But there's the rub: claims can be contested. America's national independence came at the price of blood—lives were given so that Americans might have a freer life. In turn, as Arlington Cemetery reminds us, many others have died in quest of what they conceived as freedom's ground, freedom's zone. And the pursuit of happiness has often been tainted by selfishness, with one person or group enjoying it for a while at the cost of another's unhappiness. Time has shown us, more than once, a home in upheaval.

The Jewish and Christian scriptures tell us that this has all happened before, and also that it is not the last word. In the second Book of Samuel, when David is settled into his own home after much conflict, he wishes to build a temple, a house for God, in celebration. He is told instead that God will be at home not so much in a place as in a people, though a place they shall have; and he is also told that it will be a long haul.

## Places

In Luke's Gospel, a girl in Galilee is assured that, through her keeping faith with God, a son will be born to her who will vindicate David's hope, a hope which might itself be called one for life, liberty, and the pursuit of happiness. All this is astounding to Mary, and is good news indeed; but in the event it is followed by her bearing her son away from her own home, and out of any home, in a stable. Too soon after that, she and her husband and her child are all refugees, in pursuit of security.

The memory of these events will be with many of us at this time of year. Perhaps that memory may sharpen our attention to those in this country who, for whatever reasons, have nobody to take them in. We have all hymned America as the 'home of the brave,' and long may it be so: but any country which is truly 'under God' has also to seek to be the home of the helpless, the unfortunate, the seemingly expendable ones. It is the very essence of the Bible that that is how God deals with us: and if this fades from the American dream, we will be left with a nightmare of selfishness instead.

Throughout the world, perhaps the two most widely-known images of human dwelling are the White House and the Capitol. Both stand for power, even for supreme power. But both also stand, even to people who will never set foot in America, for a hope that power will be well employed—with skill, certainly, but with compassion, and generosity, and a readiness to help make the world more than a stockade, or an armed camp, or a refuse-dump: to help make it a home. The men and women we elect will rarely persist in that aim unless we re-commission them by our own conduct. Domestic policy, like foreign policy, begins at home.

When you fly over America, as you look down the land presents itself to you as one where many promises have been fulfilled, many opportunities met. Green or gold, the miles of crops unfold, the roads thread from town to town: the land is no longer, in Frost's other words, 'unstoried, artless, unenhanced'. But success, even partial success, is something given us in trust, and conditionally. The condition is that we develop the hearts of home-makers, for all in need. If we do not, we will ourselves be aliens, for all our finery.

*Georgetown: November, 1996*

IRELAND

## *The Salmon of Wisdom*
### 32nd Sunday in Ordinary Time, Year A

IF YOU COME BACK TO THESE SHORES AFTER wandering abroad for a while, it's likely that you will find in some odd corner of your baggage, or in some remote pocket, a foreign coin or two left over. Recently I turned out an Irish coin of modest worth, and where we might have the Queen or a koala, it had a salmon. It was a salmon of considerable flair or flourish—no ordinary salmon, you might think. And indeed it isn't all ordinary, because it is a reminder of the ancient Irish belief, enshrined in one story in particular, that the salmon was the fish of wisdom: it was itself wise, and it could give wisdom to its eater.

I've never eaten enough salmon at one go to find out whether this is true or not. But the story, the yarn if you like, carries a deep and important truth, just as our Lord's parable stories do. Salmon are commonplace in Ireland—they are not dead-easy to catch, but there are a lot of them—and it is in the midst of commonplace things that wisdom is to be found. I was prompted to think of this by some phrases from our first Reading today, a reading in which it is said that 'he who watches for [Wisdom] at dawn shall not be disappointed, for he shall find her sitting by his gate', and that '[Wisdom] makes her own rounds, seeking those worthy of her, and graciously appears to them in the ways, and meets them enthusiastically.' In other words, God would have us believe that wisdom is not exotic or labyrinthine

'... the salmon was the fish of wisdom: it was itself wise, and it could give wisdom to its eater.'

or very, very rare: it is to hand. It is perhaps to hand like the fish with which so many seas and lakes and rivers teem, there for the taking.

Now this is good news, and for some of us it is surprising news, and not the easiest thing in the world to believe. For surely to God there is plenty of un-wisdom around—not just ignorance, or puzzlement, or reserved judgement, or any number of mistakes, but outright folly, which is the opposite of wisdom. I could, if you liked, keep you here all through the afternoon and well into the night with the long, long catalogue of human follies, past and present: the wasteful ones, and the dispiriting ones, and the obscene ones, and the lethal ones, and all the rest of them; and so could you keep me, if we changed places; but there is no need for all that—you get the point. Sometimes, we may feel, the nearest we get to wisdom is in the form of being cynical about folly; and that is not very high on the wisdom-register.

Still and all, the Father and the Son and the Spirit of Wisdom tell us that we can be wise, you and I, within the tissues and contours of our actual lives. Most if not all of us in this chapel have received the sacrament of Confirmation, a sacrament conceived not only as offering us bravery, but as offering us wisdom. At such a time, typically, the divine Person whose very name is Wisdom is appealed to as the One ready to infuse himself or herself into the common hours of our common days. Over the twenty centuries since the birth of Christ, his community has gone on asking for wisdom *as of right*, because we were promised by no one less than that same Christ that we would be given that Spirit, every last, least man, woman and child of us. Asking for wisdom is not crying for the moon: asking for wisdom is like asking for some fish to go with the chips of every day.

No doubt all of us remember that one of the earliest code-drawings of our Lord was that of the fish—not quite a salmon, but it might as well have been. He is, we say, our 'daily bread': he is, as it were, our 'daily fish'. In our daily lives, if we are denied food for long enough, everything else pales and is deferred until we have had something to eat; but when we have had it, life has to be resumed, and to be carried through as well as we can live it. By the same token, if we do have any enthusiasm for living wisely, if we are not the mere addicts of folly, it is fair enough for us to reach in prayer and sacrament and Christian reflection for Christ the Salmon of Wisdom—it is more than fair enough, it is indispensable. After that, though, we have to step back from this privileged stream and go walking the streets of our city, or travelling the roads and airways of our country, as people full-fed on wisdom. And whenever we falter, as falter we all will, let us take heart from the knowledge that there is always another meal to be had. This is the Salmon that does not die.

*Newman: 1996*

PRAYER

## *The Wild Prayer of Longing*

29th Sunday in Ordinary Time, Year C

IF WE ASK OURSELVES WHAT WE ARE DOING HERE today, many answers are possible. We are worshipping—that is, acknowledging that we did not originate ourselves, or give ourselves meaning, and claiming that God is not only greater than ourselves but better than ourselves. We are behaving ritually—that is, putting ourselves in tune with rhythms of the cosmos, rhythms of the past and of the present, with a view to living well in the future. We are communing—that is, sharing at least some little part of our lives with one another, not because we are forced to do so, but because this is part of the style of humanity. But I hope that we are also engaging, to some degree, in the wild prayer of longing.

'The wild prayer of longing' is a phrase from W. H. Auden. Auden is talking about the element of yearning which can be there in anyone's life, the refusing to settle for what is simply so at the moment. He thinks, or he seems to think, that this is a kind of praying—the heart searching, asking, appealing. I think that he is right. St Paul says that the Holy Spirit voices things in our hearts, 'with cries too deep for words'. I regard almost all of our hungerings and hankerings as being prayers-in-the-making, and often as actual prayers.

Those prayers may not look very respectable, and sometimes they have a very selfish aspect. Alexander is supposed to have wept because there were no more worlds for him to conquer: his hankering for conquest was not admirable. But his gifts sought expression, his energies sought outcome: he wanted not just to have more or do more but to be more; and the wish to be more is entirely admirable, just as it is entirely God-given. That wish was not just the result of his genetic endowment or of his upbringing; it was provoked by the one who brought him to be in the first place.

Few of us are Alexanders, or captains of industry, or movers and shakers, or highly theatrical in our cast or character. Few of us are 'wild', in that sense of the word. But most of us have known wild gusts of longing—desires, hopes, yearnings. Most of us have known the heart's imperatives. Too often, these cries of the heart have been regarded as a kind of babble of some internal rabble, which should be rebuked and muted as rapidly as possible. But as I see it, most of us are tempted to be too slight and feeble in our yearnings, not too ambitious.

Certainly, in the two principal readings for today's Mass, there is nothing apologetic or decorous about the longings expressed. Moses praying with outflung arms, arms which have to be kept outflung, as the story has it, if the prayer is to be granted—Moses is a man without apologies, and without reservations. In the Gospel story, the widow simply badgers the judge to the point where he gives in. Moses is a wild one, the widow is a wild one. Well, there is a Moses in our own hearts, a widow in our own hearts. Moses prays for his endangered people, and heaven knows, we know enough endangered people, and we too are of their company. The widow prays out of her personal need, and we too have personal needs, some perhaps unidentified, but many all too aching. God no more wants us to keep our needs to ourselves than, in the biblical stories, he wanted either of those figures to do so.

After we have said the Creed, we will make explicit some of our yearnings, in the Prayers of the Faithful. Most of those will be formal, which does not mean that they are a formality. But we will also pause to remember the other things we have at heart, the other persons and fortunes we hold dear. Bitter or sweet as our consciousness may be, there is likely to be a touch of wildness about it. And in the whole of the rest of the Mass, as up to this point, hardly a minute will go by without a reference to, or a dramatizing of, the heart's hungers. Here, we are not only free to express these—we are called to express them. We should take them out of this chapel as things blessed by God's company, blessed by his hearing.

They may have to be changed, and some of them will not be sated this side of the grave. But whatever we or others do about them, no good will come of denying them. Nobody ever went heartlessly to Heaven.

*Newman: November, 1992*

WISDOM

## The Light of Wisdom

IN THE TWENTIETH CENTURY THERE WAS A VERY ambitious, and very gifted, lawyer called F. E. Smith. He was in many ways a pretty distasteful individual: but whatever he may have lacked, he did abound in confidence. On one occasion, when he had been speaking in court, the judge said to him, 'Mr Smith, I have listened attentively to you for twenty minutes, and I am still none the wiser.' To this, Smith said, 'Very possibly, my Lord, but at least better informed'.

I am sorry to say that F. E. Smith went on to become Lord Birkenhead, and he lived arrogantly ever afterwards. But he was right about one thing. Being wise is *not* the same as being well-informed. This is not the first time that a passage has been chosen from the Book of Wisdom on Newman's Valete occasion, and I expect that it will not be the last. After all, the reason for the construction of this remarkable set of buildings in the first place, and the reason for its being maintained and staffed and opened and occupied as it is today, is not simply in order for it to be a kind of hostel for a predominantly Catholic group, but in order to provide a milieu in which, according to our individual abilities and our pooled abilities, we may become wiser.

This may seem an over-large claim to make, but no, my dears, it isn't. Of course it's true that wisdom is not a commodity for which one can contract. If Newman doesn't feed or house you as agreed, you can ask for your money back, and get it: but if you go away no wiser than you came in, you will be waiting a long time for the cheque. Still, openings towards wisdom are like openings towards beauty or courage or love: contexts can be provided, insight can be brought to bear, encouraging companions can be mustered, a run can be started—like a ski-run, or a marathon-run, or the run of some great piece of music, which begins with a few seemingly commonplace, tentative notes, and then winds its way right into the heart. Newman exists mainly in order to make that kind of thing feasible—to haunt us all with the hope of wisdom.

The Book of Wisdom is located between the Song of Songs and the Book of Sirach or Ecclesiasticus. The first of these is unblushingly erotic, and the second is by somebody who has seen it all, who is utterly worldly-wise. And that is where the Book of Wisdom belongs. It belongs firmly in touch with our yearnings for pleasure and happiness and fruitfulness, and firmly in touch with the world's intricate and complex ways. Real wisdom, whatever names we give to it, should always be in touch with the greening shoots which emerge in a wheatfield's early days, and with the bronzed growths which, in time, offer themselves for harvest, and so for nourishment, and so for new life.

I would be very surprised if most of you ever do university courses and find that they are advertised in terms just like these. Like F. E. Smith, most of your teachers, like most of my teachers, would aspire at best to leave you better informed. It is for you, they would think, not for them, to aspire to the green and the gold of wisdom, whenever it comes to contracts. If they are not right, at least they are realistic. For you at your age or for me at mine to make an exit from a university, or from Newman, with nothing to show for our time spent but a bunch of unremarkable transactions—social deals, pedagogical deals, a bit of comradeship here, a bit of getting smart there—for this, together with some certification or qualification to be *all* that we leave with, would be a sorry business.

For the fact is that we are *all* capable of becoming wise, every last one of us. A couple of weeks ago I heard an Australian musician on the radio say that, when he was a little boy, he got 99 out of 100 for playing the piano in some examination, and his mother took him off to the examiner to find out where he had lost the one mark. I am not talking about that kind of behaviour. Our capacity to be wise is not something which can be calibrated, and it is certainly not something for star-performers alone. Rather, the opposite of being wise is being a fool: and being a fool has nothing to do with your IQ. It has to do, usually, with being an evader of callings to personal growth. It has to do with deafening yourself to the acorn's hungering to become an oak, the embryo's hungering to become a free-standing woman or man. The American writer Thoreau, who *was* a wise person, said that, 'It is a property of wisdom not to do desperate things', and by 'desperate' he did not mean something like running around in public with lethal weapons. He meant *giving up on oneself*. He meant that the stupidest thing you can do is to write yourself off. He meant that being a blockhead, or what one might call a 'blockheart', was a matter of consenting to be a puppet on a string—the string of unconsidered hungers or of unchallenged cynicisms. He meant that when we live wisely we do not live sluggishly or compulsively or resentfully or greedily or evasively. And he never said a truer word. It is a property of wisdom not to do desperate things.

This Mass, like every Mass, reiterates that truth. We began, in ritual, by acknowledging that we have blundered around in our moral lives, and that we continue to do so. But we are not blundering when we ask of the God who fathers and mothers us into existence from instant to instant that we may blossom in insight, in realism, and in proficiency in love's ways. And we are not blundering when, in concert with the Jesus who had to learn how to love and how to be loved, we think at this moment of those who fill our pews and fill this chapel. We are wise to do these things, wise to have these hopes. And we are wisest of all if, before we do the other things this evening holds for us, we thank God and one another for our being kept somewhat on the stretch at present, somewhat given to outreach. Every crucifix you have ever seen displays stretch and outreach, displays lived wisdom in action, lived love in action. And every painting of the risen Lord proclaims that he was wise to have made those moves. At a Mass like this one, in which we farewell some of our number, we do so in the hope that they will take with them some of the heart's skills, skills in which wisdom and love are, after all, identical.

*Newman: Valete Mass, October, 1995*

DEATH

# A Raising Spirit

## 14th Sunday in Ordinary Time, Year A

IN TODAY'S PASSAGE FROM THE LETTER TO THE Romans, St Paul says, 'If the Spirit of him who raised Jesus from the dead dwells in you, then he who raised Christ from the dead will bring your mortal bodies to life also through his Spirit dwelling in you.' This is an old story: but it is still good news. Very briefly, let me say why.

St Paul supposes that everything that is mortal in us is attended by the Father of all life. When we were very young, unless things had gone badly wrong for us, we expected that someone could cope on our behalf. If it was not our father or our mother, it was somebody who acted in their stead. We did not think that to be in the world was, as the poet says, to be all 'dark and comfortless'. Gradually, we took more responsibility for our own lives, and usually we took some responsibility for the lives of others. We also learned that, from some things, no earthly father or mother could shield us. To learn just that is a precondition of maturity, of realism.

But Christ's call to us—it is voiced, among other places, in his own prayer which we will shortly say together again—Christ's call to us is to find that child-heart again, in our maturity, in our mortality, in our aging and declining, as well as in our flourishing. The gospel tells us that when he was young he already knew that he had to be about his Father's business; later, he too had to re-embrace

'... Christ's call to us is to find that
child-heart again, in our maturity,
in our mortality, in our aging and
declining, as well as in our flourishing.'

being about his Father's business, about the cherishing of a wounded world, even though he had now had many disappointments.

And so it goes with us. We too, in spite of disappointments and disconcerments, have to keep turning back to God our Father, asking him that our spirit may be his Spirit, that his lavishness with love may, in some degree, become our lavishness too. God does not do cosmetic surgery, does not give face-lifts or golden hair in place of silver: God is not averse from our mortal ways and courses; God does not have misgivings about time. What he does do, if we want him to, and if we turn to him with a steady hope, is to bring our mortal hearts to immortal life. He wants to give us not just what he has, but who he is: he does want his Spirit, which is also the Spirit of Jesus, to be our Spirit too. This is the thing we most need: and this is the thing which we should most wish for one another.

*Newman: 1999*

# *The Confused and the Evil*

### 32nd Sunday in Ordinary Time, Year C

MANY OF YOU WILL HAVE DIPPED INTO THAT VERY peculiar volume, Jonathan Swift's *Gulliver's Travels*. In some versions it can look like a children's book, mainly because all of the grim and drastic stuff has been cut out, and all the cute stuff has been left in. The result can be charming, indeed enchanting, and I hope that the pruned-down version goes on being re-published.

But what Swift was really up to was writing a political and social satire, something fierce and edged. It is not what one would call a genial piece of work. Swift took the view that the public scene was littered with those whom he called, succinctly, 'knaves and fools'. He thought that we would be fortunate indeed, blessed in fact, to escape untainted from their influence. Now you may say that Swift's view of affairs was coloured by the Irish climate, or by the foiling of his ambitions, or by some other passing thing. But St Paul lived in a warmer climate than Swift, and he had the spectacular career of a premier apostle, and he was good at not being panicked by passing events. And he does say in today's reading from the second letter to the Christians at Thessalonica, 'Pray that we may be delivered from confused and evil men', which sounds to me pretty close to Swift's 'knaves and fools'. And if St Paul were drafting a letter today to the Christians of Melbourne, I don't think that he would be inclined to change his instructions.

The group of us in this chapel at this moment might argue about who are the evil men (and women), who the confused men (and women). But nobody who is not terminally absent-minded could deny that both lots abound. If we could send out sound-waves or radio-waves from where we sit together, their expanding circumferences would take in a greater and greater array of them. Along with all the 'sweetness and light' of which Swift also spoke so memorably, there would be some liars and cheats, there would be some violent brutalizers, and somewhere else would be the sheerly selfish predators who use fear, or sexual demand, or the whiplash of power to make others so many toys in their own game. These people are not devils: they are, well—people. They are morally stupified people, morally twisted people. You can see or hear or read about them in the news every day. From time to time, you may have to go home to one of them.

What to do? Sometimes, there is much that we can do. There may be things to be confronted, messy emotions to be worked through, a price to be paid in our own disturbance. It may take a long time, with blunders likely and tears aplenty: but sometimes things can be changed, and sometimes it is we who can change them. Most of the saints we have ever heard of, and all of the apostles, had to make some radical change in their lives, and it is mainly because they consented to do so that we remember them. Let us never underestimate the importance of making what changes for the better we can in our own lives, or in the lives of others. Nothing is more important than that.

But even if we are baffled as to what moves to make, or what changes to hope for, we can linger on the first word of St Paul's directive: '*Pray* that we may be delivered from confusion and evil [from folly and knavery].' Surely, when he speaks in this vein, he is simply echoing those words of our Lord which we have all spoken times without number, and which we shortly will say again, when we ask that our Father 'deliver us from evil'. It is true that some evils are so ancient that we can think of them as inevitable, and some are so new that we can scarcely identify them. Either way, prayer can freshen both our minds and our hearts, and can fortify our resolve. It is not our business to go the way of Swift's fantasy, whether in its adult version or in its childish version. It is our business to take the path of our Father, a path beyond confusion and beyond evil.

*Newman: November, 1995*

HATRED

# *The Wars of Love*
### 5th Sunday of Lent, Year A

THE AUSTRALIAN POET JAMES MCAULEY ENDS ONE of his poems with the words, 'Turn back and fight the wars of love.' Now McAuley was a pugnacious man, but even so you might jib at such a directive. 'What', you might ask, 'has love to do with wars, or wars with love?' With enough love there would be no wars, and vice versa. Isn't McAuley just being perverse in putting things in that way?

The episode in today's Gospel, the raising of Lazarus, might prompt us to think again. Four times in the full story, as John tells it, the word 'love' or the adjective 'loved' occurs: indeed this is a lovestory, though not what we usually understand by that expression. The fortunes of love are related, the tests of love spelled out.

What we have to remember about the Lazarus story is that eventually Jesus will pay for Lazarus's life with his own life. For immediately after the account of our Lord's loving miracle, John tells us that it is precisely on account of this that there is a state conspiracy against him, a conspiracy to bring about his death: and it is, as we know, to be a successful conspiracy. After this, Jesus is a man watching his back, a man on the run. But it is no use: and because he will not change his ways, it is all over very soon.

You see, love does have wars. The world is in many ways better and more beautiful than we can possibly say, though artists and others keep on trying to say it: but it is also affronted and savaged by evil influences, which both lodge in the hearts of human beings, and become ingrained in the structures of society. Those influences—which our Lord went so far as to attribute to 'the ruler of this world', meaning not his heavenly Father but the devil who rejoices in our unhappiness and destruction—those influences have to be tackled again and again, day by day. We will, in a few minutes, pray to that heavenly Father both that he give us the food we need each day, and that he forgive us the animosities which we are all prone to level against someone else, or many other people. Such a prayer is not only an act of obedience to the Jesus who told us to say it: it is a piece of realism about the world we inhabit, and the proneness we all have to cave in before the forces of cynicism and scorn, self-promotion or self-laceration.

It did not come as a surprise to Jesus that he should be hated. It is only in fairy-tales or in fantasies that 'all the world loves a lover'. In the real world, where opportunism has many faces, and anger can easily be flicked on the raw, and profiteering is the name of the game for everybody who makes a hate-filled X-rated movie, or preys on the agonies of people addicted to hard drugs: in the real world, where we can be calloused against the distresses which, quite certainly, we will all see within the next week: in the real world, where we are likely to throw God, our primal lover and daily sustainer, at best a few scraps of prayer before we return to more important matters than our source and our destination: in that real world, which Jesus inhabited, as he still inhabits it, it is no surprise that he should be hated.

I am not saying these things in some cheap play for self-disgust, or to increase the sum of mournfulness in the world. Self-disgust is of the devil, not of God: and there is too much mournfulness already. But I am trying to keep faith with our Lord's rousing his sympathetic watchers and hearers to see that the power of his Father can indeed be called upon to defeat deathly forces in our hearts and in our world. He did this in all sobriety, with much realism. He did not immortalize Lazarus: Lazarus would have to die, as would Jesus his dear friend, and as we all have to do. But there are deaths and deaths; and although our physical death is a bad business, the death of the spirit, the corrosion and befouling of the heart, is much worse still: so much so, that a man or a woman may well choose physical death in order to have life of the spirit—which was of course what Jesus himself did, and is what the many martyrs, most of them unknown, have done over the centuries.

Jesus was unique, but he refused to be alone: indeed, part of his uniqueness is in the thoroughness with which he refused the option of being alone, in the sense of being aloof or self-sufficient. In a few moments, we will say that it was 'for us and for our salvation' that he lived his life, died his death, and was brought unkillably to life once more in what we call his resurrection. 'For *us* and for our salvation': not for himself. In fact, had he been determined to go only his own way and be only his own theme, he would not have been raised, and none of us would be in this chapel today. His was indeed a war of love, and we have all been inducted into his company for that campaign.

Much later, well into the bitter-sweet fortunes of a world which knew his name but kept forgetting his meaning, a preacher like myself, but a very great one, John Donne, reflected on his mortality—the mortality in which he was bonded with Jesus and with Lazarus, with you and with me. He thought of a bell like the one I rang a little while ago to remind you of this Mass, only Donne's bell was the one rung when someone had died. And, musing on our solidarity with one another, and of the perpetual call to us to campaign once again for love, he wrote,

> No man is an Iland, intire of it selfe;every man is a peece of the Continent, a part of the maine; if a Clod bee washed away by the Sea, Europe is the lesse, as well as if a Promontorie were, as well as if a Mannor of thy friends or of thine owne were; any mans death diminishes me, because I am involved in Mankinde; and therefore never send to know for whom the bell tolls; It tolls for thee.

Words like these might have been words for Lazarus; and if they were, they should have pressed him beyond words into deeds. They are in fact words for us too: and they take us into the wars of love.

*Newman: March, 1996*

## THE UNIVERSITY

# On Taking Experience Seriously

### 18th Sunday in Ordinary Time, Year A

TODAY'S GOSPEL TALKS ABOUT ONE OF THE miracles of Jesus, a miracle which, like all the rest of them, has to do with opening out the vistas and prairies and starfields of life. But in fact I want to say a word not directly about that text, but about the sentence that precedes it. We are told, there, that when he and his friends heard about the execution of his cousin John the Baptizer, they went out of action for a while, in a quiet place. This morning, I am saying a word in favour of the policy of going out of action for a while.

Some of you, if you think about it for a moment, may be surprised by this. After all, I earn my keep as a university teacher; and even the youngest of you must by now have realized that teachers have often to be trying to get people into action. It can seem, sometimes, as if the world is full of reasons why books have not been read, essays have not been written, and the contracts made when people undertook courses have not been kept. I assure you, I am not naive about these matters. But I am talking about something a little different. I am talking about the need to savour experience, and digest it, and be thoroughly nourished by it.

More than once, I have read that when we see goldfish swimming around in a bowl, we should not be too concerned on their behalf, since their memory-span is so short that each time they come round again it is, as it were, a fresh adventure. Experience is com-

'... when we see goldfish swimming around in a bowl, we should not be too concerned on their behalf, since their memory-span is so short that each time they come round again it is, as it were, a fresh adventure.'

pletely wasted on them: they live practically instantaneously. Whether we like it or not, we are not just like that. Or are we?

I think that a lot of us, a lot of the time, act as if we have goldfish-blood in us. We move through life with a minimum of remembering, sorting-out, and sizing-up. Our bowl may be bigger than the goldfish's bowl—may be the great globe itself—but our style can be just the same as the fish's; circling, cycling, revising nothing, pressing on.

If we were to have second thoughts about such a way of going on, there might be a weekday reason, and there might be a Sunday reason. The weekday reason is that most of what any university is to do with is the learning from experience: and the Sunday reason is that what most of what Christianity is to do with is, also, learning from experience.

Universities exist for the generating and the assessing of intellectual experience. Research which is not in a real sense experience is bogus research: teaching and learning which are not in a real sense experience are failed teaching, failed learning. And built into research, teaching and learning is an element of assessment of experience—sizing it up, challenging it, appraising and evaluating. Not to engage in that process is to be at a university under false pretences. By that criterion, quite a lot of people are at universities under false pretences. But quite a lot more deserve to be there, and they honour the institutions by their presence. I presume that this is true of most of you.

What I call 'the Sunday reason' for not living like a goldfish is that Christianity exists as a way of fostering experience and as a way of assessing it. In some Christian traditions, men and women assess their lives daily, and more than daily, on the assumption that something significant is always going on—that the Holy Spirit of God is constantly astir in their hearts, and that they are constantly consenting to the Spirit's creative stirrings, or resisting those stirrings. This is a good policy. It is realistic, it is itself creative, and it certainly beats being a goldfish.

*Newman: August, 1993*

COMPASSION

## *Praying in a Certain Place*

17th Sunday in Ordinary Time, Year C

'AND IT CAME TO PASS, THAT, AS HE WAS PRAYING in a certain place, when he ceased, one of his disciples said unto him, "Lord teach us to pray."' St Luke does not specify the place, and it scarcely matters to us today. But I want to dwell for a few moments on the notion of 'praying in a certain place'. All of us live in time and space. We can be very conscious of *time* as a determinant in our lives. Deadlines, timetables, seasons, phases in development, reaching crucial moments, running out of time. Some of you came in late for this Mass, and some of you are waiting for it to be over. All of us plan for tomorrow, yearn for it, fear it, have to deal with it. We were time-bound, from the moment of our conception.

But we also think a lot about space and place. We ask to be given space, and for other people to get out of our space. We want very much to have access to certain places, and we emphatically do not want to go to others. Generations of Newman students have almost worn a groove in the footpath to the Clyde Hotel, but there's no groove on the way to the cemetery. And because we are so space-determined, so place-minded, this has become a source of metaphors for our understanding our own attitudes and outlooks. 'Marlboro Country' and 'Kingswood Country' are not literal localities: they are countries of the mind. They embody wants and preferences. The Australia or America or England or Greece or Thailand that people argue about are not only patches of geography: they are configurations of attitude. Songs like 'Everybody Gets to Go to the Moon', or 'Flying down to Rio', or 'New York, New York', or 'I Still Call Australia Home' are ways of going to countries of the heart.

So when St Luke says that Jesus was 'praying in a certain place', we might rephrase this as, 'Jesus was praying out of a certain place'—praying out of a certain country of the mind and of the heart. When we pray, in one sense we go somewhere else, somewhere different from the land of the pragmatic and the functional in which most of us spend most of our time. It isn't 'somewhere else' in the sense of being out of touch, disconnected from the actual, a fantasy. It is in fact more in touch with the actual. It is the land of unselfishness, the land of no more lies, the country of confrontation. Much of our life is lived in a milieu of deferral, procrastination, hedging, chancing things unreasonably, self-preoccupation, and fear. A great Australian historian said once that the enemies of seriousness in the intellectual life are frittering, pottering, and gadding. All of that belongs to the territory of the trivial, and most of us go there pretty often, if we don't actually live there. The land of prayer is much more grown up, much more adequately human. To pray is to consent to spit the dummy, to climb out of the creche, to grow as a self.

When Jesus prayed, and taught us to pray, he was doing two things. He was entrusting himself to the Begetter of the universe, and he was giving himself in compassion to his sisters and brothers throughout time and space. What we call the 'Our Father' or the 'Lord's Prayer' faces at once into all that has ever surrounded and determined the fortunes of the human race, and into the lives of individual men and women. It frames an act of confidence in the goodness of the God who made and makes us, it articulates our shared need, and it declares a resolve to be creative on behalf of others. The name of the 'certain place' of prayer is, in other words, 'Compassion'. In that country of the mind and heart, one sees that our universe is not an anonymous, indifferent milieu, but the homeland and the heartland of God. And at the same time, one sees that God the life-cherisher calls all of us to be life-cherishers and life-givers in concert with him. We ask for food, and forgiveness, because we need them both. We agree to offer food, and forgiveness, because others need them both. If we mean what we say, prayer will send us back, a little shaken but more than a little heartened, to the tasks of everyday. And after all, we are not determined either by the Clyde Hotel or by the cemetery. The country of compassion can be, and should be, wherever we happen to be.

*Newman: July, 1992*

HOME

# Roads and Lodgings

## 5th Sunday of Easter, Year A

SOMEWHERE IN AMERICA—I FORGET WHERE—there is a travel agency called, 'Please Go Away'. It is an agreeably catchy title. Of course they want you to travel, and of course they know that you will need a little persuasion. Somewhat in the same vein, motels which know what is good for them inform their patrons of check-out time. Of course they want you to come in, and of course they want you to keep moving, so that others can come in. It is the business of the travel agency and of the motel alike to keep us enthusiastic for moving on.

On the other hand, plenty of Australians who have never clapped eyes on Melbourne will have learned at school that John Batman said, upon seeing it, that this was the 'spot for a village'. Batman did not propose to be a perpetual rover, however good he may have been at travelling. He wanted there to be a settlement, and perhaps a city: and here we are, vindicating his wish. In the same way, once we had put dogs and apes and eventually human beings into space, sooner or later we were going to build lodgings for them. Beyond the troposphere and the stratosphere, in that weirdly foreign locale, pretty soon we will have motels in space.

We do these things partly because we have twin appetites—appetites for roads and for homes. We want to change, and we want to have something to change for. In today's Gospel, both of those appetites are recognized. Our Lord says to his apostles, and through them to us, that he is 'going to prepare a place' for us. It's not just a question of making a reservation, but of establishing a home. And within a couple of sentences he is saying that he is himself 'the way'. Goal and method, point of arrival and pathway—he holds out to all of us the prospect of both.

He is speaking in metaphor, which is a concentrated way of telling the truth, and we can find less concentrated ways of 'reading off' the metaphor for ourselves. Later in the history of Christianity, the talk about *destination* would be read off as if it meant, simply, the heavenly home, something to be found beyond death's dark door. And the talk about the *way* would be read off as if it referred always and only to the Christian Church, and in fact the Catholic Church. I am not saying anything about those questions at this moment. I want instead to make a point made, I think, by the whole of the New Testament. It is this.

It is possible for us to go all-out for only one of the God-given appetites, possible to idolize transience or to idolize permanence. Neither of these, by itself, takes seriously God's real creativity, or our real possibilities. If we think that only novelty matters, that shift and show and flair are the only things to invest in, we are selling short our capacity for fidelity, for being substantial persons, for acting as selves instead of as fluctuating clouds. If, on the other hand, we praise only the established, the familiar, the perpetual, we are refusing to keep faith with that biological and psychological and social creativity which brought us all the way from being specks of organic material to the striking individuals that we are today. Yes, we are home-bodies, but we are also trail-blazers—after all, nobody but you has taken the path to where you are right now. Yes, we flower individually, but the family tree that bears us is rooted in the earth.

What has that to do with Christianity? This: Jesus came to reconcile us not only to one another—which God knows we need—but to the primal facts of our existence, the conditions of being human. That we are sexual, and that we are mortal, are famous among those facts—and we are sexual because we are mortal. An enormous amount of the folly, criminality, vice, waste, self-destruction, and destruction of others, comes from the fact that most of us are only partly reconciled to being this particular human being, and being human at all.

We resent the fixities which are essential to us, or we resent the changes which are essential to us. We give all sorts of names to our discontents and arguments, but in the end the quarrel is with God. In some degree, every person in this chapel at this moment has a quarrel with God. That is what we confessed at the beginning of this Eucharist. That was what was addressed in Christ's dying and rising. And that was what he was pointing to when, the night before he died, he offered himself as both the way to change and the home-maker for our yearnings.

*Newman: May, 1993*

EUCHARIST

## *She'll Be Right*
### 17th Sunday in Ordinary Time, Year A

YEARS AGO, I HEARD SOMEBODY SAY THAT THERE is an expression which strikes horror and dismay into the heart of people proposing to invest in some Australian venture; the expression is, 'She'll be right.' The implication was that our national proneness to say these words—often with the footnote, 'No worries!'—is liable to signal a slapdash attitude, a 'what-the-hell-couldn't-careless' dismissiveness about problems and challenges and even the possibility of outright disaster.

Now I don't know whether we are, as a people or nation, more like this than other peoples or nations, and in fact I suspect that we're less so than some others; it's not hard to get a fierce argument going in Australia, if you know your time and place and group. But the reason I raise the matter is that St Paul, in a reading today, could sound like a very early northern-hemisphere Australian. In his letter to the Christian converts in Rome, he says, 'We know that God makes all things work together for the good of those who have been called according to his decree.' It sounds a bit like 'No worries!': it sounds a bit like 'She'll be right.'

Because after all, you and I believe that we are amongst 'those who have been called according to his decree'. We are here, in this handsome but culturally odd building in the middle of a perfectly good day off, only because we are convinced that God has called us here—our behaviour makes no sense at all, otherwise. But what about St Paul's claim that God is, in just our lives, in just this place and time, making things work together for our good?

Each of us can consult her heart, or his, about this question; but there is no denying that it really doesn't look this way in the short run. There is the small-time stuff, of course—how many of us have had a perfect run through this morning, or, failing that, through the last week? But there is also the heavy-duty stuff, which can range all the way from things that steadily drain our energies to things that break our hearts. The first time I ever set foot in this University, one night in the early 'sixties, a distinguished Australian poet and intellectual told me in public that he thought that I needn't worry about going to find distress, because distress would probably come and find me. He was right: it did; it does for all of us; and often it does not feel as if God is orchestrating pain's dark music.

What we make of this, and what we do about it, is emphatically up to each of us, individually. To continue the autobiographical note for a moment, in this same spot I have witnessed adults being received into the Church, and others being married: others, in this Chapel, I have helped the Christian community to bury. All of them were people I loved. But every last one of them had to decide what attitude they would adopt to what is proclaimed in St Paul's teaching in today's reading. Because when you do get down to the bottom line, either you do believe that God is the weaver, or the navigator, or the orchestrator, or the pacer, or some metaphor like that, or your claiming to be a Christian is just a piece of absent-mindedness. A God who does not steer our ways might just as well be a piece of seaweed.

To be glib about this is witless, or dishonourable, or both. Human history is disfigured by vilenesses for which no words are adequate, and some of them are taking place right now, near and far. But any time you have walked into a Catholic church, whether it was a hut or was Chartres Cathedral, you saw a crucial thing: you saw the crucifix. My contentious friend Daniel Berrigan said many years ago that it might be good for us if, when we came to Mass on Sunday, we saw above the altar, instead of a crucifix, a representation of a black man in an electric chair. He was writing in America, and of America, but I think that you get the point. The crucifix always stands for seemingly meaningless, seemingly unjust, pain inflicted on anyone upon whom it may lodge.

In other words, no one less or other than the Son of God lodges deep at the heart of our own personal distresses, whatever they may be. He, the One who beams into our short-sighted vision, the Image of God our loving Father—he does so as the One for whom life and death have become intolerably dark, so dark in fact that he had to die. But he is also the One whom we name in this ritual as the Light-bringer, the bearer of bread and wine and good heart, out of the darkness. He emerges from death's tomb, death's cavern, to claim that even death works, after all.

What Jesus does *not* do is explain. He claims, and proclaims, but he does not explain. Somebody once called the poet Ezra Pound, 'the village explainer', meaning by this, I suppose, that you could only get away with his explanations in the confined space of a village. This is not the way of Jesus. Rather, putting before us the bread and wine which also present his very Self, he claims that all that is deathly in our experience can be made lively by his Father. It is up to each of us, sustained by the prayers of our sisters and brothers, to take him at his word, or not.

*Newman: 28 July, 1996*

SICKNESS

## *Need and Gratitude*
### 28th Sunday in Ordinary Time, Year C

YEARS AGO, I WOKE UP ONE MORNING, AND found that my face was puffy and itchy. I went to see my doctor, who said, 'You've got mumps.' He packed me off to Fairfield Infectious Diseases Hospital, not that mumps is the worst thing in the world, but because he didn't want it running wild through a large religious community of young males. So I turned up there with a supply of pyjamas (which they took away from me) and a copy of Gibbon's *Decline and Fall of the Roman Empire* (which they let me keep), and I settled down to wait things out.

I survived without incident, and here we are. But while I was there I saw two fellow-patients whom I have never forgotten. One of them was a man who was in the next ward, just a glass partition away. His wife travelled a long way each day to see him, and she sat with him: he was highly energetic, but there was no way on God's earth that he would ever recognize her again. He had had an infection in the lining of his brain, and he was like nothing so much as a very cheerful monkey. And this heroic woman sat there, day after day, masking her grief with smiles. I felt as if I were myself a kind of moral primitive compared with her. She was only on the other side of the glass, but she might as well have been in another of God's realms as far as I was concerned.

The other patient was someone who was carried in from an

ambulance. They took him past my bed, and I asked what his problem was, and they told me that, apart from having survived the dangers of being a fugitive here by boat, he had both TB and leprosy. They said that it would all be all right: that the leprosy could be handled, and so could the TB. I might as well go back to the *Decline and Fall of the Roman Empire*. So I did: but I did not forget him, as you see at this moment.

You know why I am telling this little story; it is because of our passage today from the Gospel, that Gospel which speaks of the ten healed lepers. This passage is from St Luke, who was by Christian report a doctor. In the seventeenth century, there was a colloquial saying in England which went, 'St Luke was a saint, and a physician, but he is dead.' It was realistic then, as it is now: even that odious man Lenin said one true thing, which is, 'In the end, we are all dead.' St Luke, like any other doctor, had mortality on his mind, and this colours his choice of incidents when he offers his impressions of our Lord in action.

What we have to remember, when these nameless ten file through our minds today, is that each of them was as exposed as the leprous and consumptive refugee who was carried past my bed—and that, then, there was no way at all that human resources could cure him. And we also have to remember that, in those days, that very leprosy took every sufferer into another zone of social being—as distant, as 'othered', as the poor man beyond the glass partition, and beyond common human contact, even from someone who loved him as much as, say, a wife might. God knows, and God knew then, that only God could help them.

And so God did, in Jesus his only Son. So long away in time, and so far away in place, we can and should thank God for that today. We are glad even when people we do not know at all are rescued from collapsed buildings, or from shipwreck: and it is right for us to be touched by this old story today. But, my brothers and sisters, it is more right still for us to be touched that the Jesus who healed these men, grateful or not, should have an eye to us, an ear for us, right now.

We have ourselves made a good move in our being here at all today: for to the Lord's question, 'Where are the grateful ones, now that they have been healed?', we can say, truly, 'Yes, *Eucharist* means *saying thank you*, and here we are *at* this Eucharist, here we are *as* this Eucharist. We might have been elsewhere on this Melbourne day, but there is enough gratitude in our hearts for your giving us life, and sustaining us in life, and teaching us love, and leading us to love better—there is enough gratitude in us to warrant our being gathered into this act of your grateful Church, an act made on behalf of a world which is only intermittently grateful.'

This Chapel, like this College, was built about a lifetime ago by people who knew instinctively that the God to whom we try to give our hearts was a God who has first given us *his* heart. He, the source of all vitality, pours it out to us, needy as we all are from day to day. So let us pray today for those benefactors, who have put a roof over our heads, and walls within which we may receive God's best gift of all, the presence of Jesus his Son. Let us take very seriously the plight of that wounded human community, which continues to bear nothing less than the wounds of Christ himself. And let us pray to be resolute and generous when it comes to tending the more or less than ten that God puts in our keeping. They will not always be grateful, but they will always be his.

*Newman: October, 1995*

DECISIONS

## *Day and Hour*
### 33rd Sunday in Ordinary Time, Year A

I CAME ACROSS A TURKISH SAYING THE OTHER DAY, and this is how it runs: 'When the axe came into the forest, the trees said: the handle is one of us.' The trees were right so far as they went, but ( so the saying implies) there was more to the situation than at first appears. When axes come into forests, it is reckoning-time for trees.

This saying might have cropped up in the second of our readings today, in which St Paul, speaking of 'the day of the Lord', the reckoning-day, says that it will come 'like a thief in the night', or like the delivery-time of a pregnant woman. Up until then it may have been a matter of business as usual, but there comes a crucial moment beyond which nothing is 'as usual,' a critically decisive moment.

Now except for the very daring ones among us, who are likely to be few, this is disconcerting, and we may well feel that it is not fair. After all, once we get beyond that junior stage in life in which pretty well everything is organized for us and provision is made for us, we probably have to put a lot of time and energy just into 'coping'—coping physically and socially and emotionally and morally. If we were to pause now for a couple of minutes, the odds are that any of us could think of several kinds of unfinished business in our lives, some of them trivial, some of them vital, most of them in between. We easily tell one another that there aren't enough hours in the day or months in the year: and it is the easiest thing in the world to feel that there are not enough years in a lifetime.

## Bread for the Journey

The more strongly we feel like this, the more disconcerting may be talk of axes in forests, or thieves in the night, or women in labour. And yet, nothing is more central to the Christian story, past present or to come, than this stress on moments of confrontation, moments of decision. The Gospels themselves are a tissue of this kind of thing. Anonymous sufferers—the blind, the bleeding, those riddled with demons—and the great ones of the earth—a Herod, a Caiphas, a Pilate—and those nearest and dearest to Jesus who have become what we might call Christian celebrities—his mother, his foster-father, his aunt and uncle and cousin, those adult intimates his disciples and apostles: the whole lot of them are presented to us in the Gospels as rising, or failing to rise, to occasions which none of them had chosen, at least in quite the forms those occasions assumed.

More than that, we are here at this Mass, as at any other Mass, to remember the ways in which Jesus rose to grossly confronting occasions in his own life, and above all to the mortal strife which took away the life of this best of human beings. Had that been the end, none of us would be here today—we have nothing running for any other two-thousand-year-old defeated peasant. We are here, though, because such was the calibre of Jesus' response to an unwanted emergency, that it unleashed a flood of creative love to benefit every conceivable world at every conceivable time.

When, in this 'Gratitude Moment' (which is what 'Eucharist' means), we receive the good food of Christ's continued presence, we are drinking to his creative deeds, and feeding off them, just as he wanted us to do. In so doing, we take in, and take on, something of his character, something of his style, his energy, his intent, his commitment. We take on, that is, something of his readiness and his power to deal lovingly and creatively with the axes in our lives, the things that go against our grain, the things that tend to intimidate our love, and drain our hope, and make mock of our faith. We have come to the right place, at the right time. And we will leave with a charge to live more heartily, more lovingly, in every one of our places, and at every one of our times.

*Newman: November, 1996*

WORDS

## *At the Tip of Our Tongue*

16th Sunday in Ordinary Time, Year A

APART FROM THE LANGUAGE WE ARE BROUGHT UP in, it's a chancy business remembering bits and pieces of any language. I knew a man once who claimed that he could say in Swahili, 'I have two oranges,' but even if he was right about this, it seems a pretty slender base for further conversation. And I'm in the same situation so far as speaking German goes. From watching old war movies, I can tell you how to hold your hands up, and from inching my way along through tourist books I can apologize to you, or ask for half a litre of beer: but after that, I'm at the mercy of the charitable German-speaking hearer.

But I do remember this: I remember that there's a German word for 'something that's at the tip of your tongue'. And even though I don't have that word at the tip of my tongue, I remembered that it existed when I was thinking about the second of our readings today. There, you will remember, St Paul says to us frankly, outright, that on the whole we are not much good at praying. Somebody might argue that he doesn't quite say that—that what he says is only that if we don't, this time round, pick up the slack in our praying, another force or person will pick up the slack. But I think that that would be mere quibbling. Good heavens—who of us would claim to be, on the whole, a *skilled* pray-er? Surely we pray as we are, and from where we are; and that means that we deliver the goods of prayer in the way that we deliver the other goods in life—provisionally, with distractions, in a self-interested fashion, and with some blurring. My mother, who is eighty-three, reports to me that her grand-daughter, who is seven, appeals in defensive argument against my brother, by saying that 'as Grandma says, we all have our own peculiarities'. Young Catherine is right—we do have our own peculiarities, and not only in our dealings with one another, but also in our dealings with God.

And our oddest peculiarity is our suspicion that there is one right thing, one truly telling thing, one decisively persuasive thing, to be said to God. It is as if, after we have said whatever good things are regularly said in our prayers, and after whatever cries we can mount in emergencies, there is, as it were, the king-hit prayer, the finally-charming phrase, the disposition of our minds and hearts such that God would have to concede that we have got it right, and therefore would have to play our lives by some tune that we have selected.

As soon as I put things like that, you see how silly it sounds. It is silly not only because we know that we cannot twirl the maker of heaven and earth around our fine logical fingers, but because we all know that life's reality, and therefore its meaning, is far denser than that. Soon we will all say together the Lord's Prayer, a prayer still warm from the lips of Jesus, a prayer in which on the one hand He salutes and prays for the doing of his Father's will, and at the same time prays for pragmatic outcomes—that people be fed, daily, which seems harmless enough: but also that we forgive those who trespass against us, which is a challenging policy indeed for sundry women, children, and men in, say, Bosnia, Northern Ireland, Burundi, Burma, or Moscow District today.

The essential thing I want to say to you today, my dears, is that we should simply open our hearts, and from time to time our mouths, to talk to our God. What particular thing we pray about, and how we pray about it, is on the whole of no great significance. Our Lord Jesus, whose fleshed-out reality we will make our own with hands and mouths this morning, this same Jesus gives Paul the good word to say that, through the stumbling and bumbling of our pleas—which includes the stumbling and bumbling of this Mass—the Good Spirit of God will take all those things which are at the tip of our tongues—the tongues of our minds, the tongues of our hearts—and will bless them through and through.

Jesus in the Garden of Gethsemene did the best he could, pleading that disgrace and death might be taken away. He prayed, and on the face of it it, it didn't work—his enemies caught up with him, and he died. In other words, he did his compassion for us mortal lot the hard way. But he kept on talking to the One who fathered his being, and found himself raised in splendour as a result of that trusting prayer.

In some parts of America, there is each weekday a very brief program on the radio which concludes with its presenter's saying, 'Be well, do good work, and keep in touch.' We cannot always guarantee being well, or guarantee doing good work: but with the Lord's help, we can undertake to keep in touch—to keep in touch with him, in our murmured prayers, and to keep in touch with our sisters and brothers, who need those prayers.

*Newman: July, 1996*

ANGELS

# Angels and Others

### 3rd Sunday of Easter, Year A

I DON'T KNOW WHETHER YOU'VE NOTICED THIS, but angels have been having a good run of it lately. I went into a bookshop in another country a couple of years ago, and there was a whole section devoted to them—right up there with food, and travel, and sex, and biography. You would think that they mattered.

And so they do, of course, though perhaps not for the reasons imagined by the publishers. They matter, in Jewish and in Christian tradition, because they are what their name means in Greek—they are messengers, they bring the good word of God. All of the finery and tenderness and general razzmatazz with which they have been surrounded by artists of various kinds is of some value only for that reason. Whenever you get a real angel, you have a summoning presence who calls us, in God's name, to 'get real'—to come to our senses, and to turn to God's radiant presence.

Being a fan of angels, I have one in my room at the University of Melbourne. At least, I have a fine framed print of an angel imagined by the incomparable Jan van Eyck, some centuries ago. This splendid fellow is the Angel Gabriel, and he is telling our Lady that she is not going to be just one of the forgotten thousands of millions of Earth's inhabitants: she is going to mother the Jesus who, with his Father and his Spirit, brought Earth and everything else to be— including the angels.

'... *a poem about death in Africa, death in Ireland, death all over our battered globe. Its title refers to a dog's grieving at a death.*'

## Bread for the Journey

Now nobody can really paint an angel, but Van Eyck has had a good try. His painting is one of the great works of western civilization. Gabriel looks, even for an angel, a very distinguished being indeed, whether you think of his rainbow wings or his splendid cloak or his exhilarated face: our Lady has the sort of robe for which you would pay a fortune if you had one: and their milieu is correspondingly up-market. I sit at my desk, and teach my students, and am very pleased to see them there.

But on another wall of the room, quite deliberately, I have another framed piece to challenge this first one. The second piece is a poster-sized print of a poem by Seamus Heaney, the current Nobel Prize winner, a poem about death in Africa, death in Ireland, death all over our battered globe. Its title refers to a dog's grieving at a death. It too, in its way, is a beautiful as well as a touching thing, and I like it all the more since it is the gift of friends. It is possible that some student may wonder what the two of them, the Van Eyck and the Heaney, are doing up there, at angles to each other.

Well, they are there essentially because of what is being talked about in today's Gospel passage. In it, you remember, the wounded former followers of Jesus, shell-shocked by his betrayal and murder, acknowledge that some women have been putting around the rumour that he is up and about again; that, having been as dead as crucifixion and a spear-thrust to the heart can get you, he is none the less to hand. This is, in the name of a book written by the sociologist Peter Berger, *A Rumor of Angels*. The whole of Christianity hinges on whether or not that is a true rumour. St Paul says, 'If Christ is not risen, our faith is vacuous', and of course he is right about this. Christ's teachings can be quarried for good ethical advice and lyrical exhortations, and I begrudge nobody any of that: but that is not what Christianity stands by, or stands for. If Christ could not take the sting out of death so that, like a bee deprived of its sting, it itself dies, the whole affair is fraudulent. The rumour-bearing angels are talking in this vein, talking by that standard. If they could not talk resurrection, then they had nothing to say.

That is why the Van Eyck is in my room. I like a masterpiece to tell the truth, and a truth that matters. And you believe, as I believe, that when Mary consented to mother God's Son, she was also mothering us all into unquenchable life, unless, by some monstrous perversity, any of us declined such an outcome. I am on the side of the angels. But I do not believe that angels come cheap. The literal painting by Van Eyck did not. It was owned by national rulers, including a Czar, it was bought for a fortune, and God knows what it is insured for. But far more importantly, it is only a heart-lifting thing on a wall unless the angel can deal with the death-afflicted dog. Angels may hearten us, but death dogs us, and here we are, squarely in the middle.

Our gospel passage this morning offers us a Jesus who has indeed been dogged to death, whose heart goes out to friends who are at present similarly dogged. Their eating together, as we will shortly eat together, is partly a re-fuelling for further steps on life's journey, but it is also an act of defiant faith—of what a deservedly celebrated poet calls 'spitting in the eye of death'. What we are saying to one another, by being here at this stylized meal, with its storytelling, and its food, and its lights and its sharing, is that while we sometimes have a dog's howl at all that is deathly, we also have an angel's flair for all that is lively. Not a bad moment, this, to pray for help from any angel on the wing.

*Newman: April, 1996*

PASSION

# *The Ointment and the Vinegar*
**Passion Sunday, Year B**

COUNTLESS TIMES, SINCE ARTISTS HAVE TRIED TO represent the passion and death of the Lord, they have found in the Gospel text what we might call eloquent items. We can see many of these picked up in any version of the Stations of the Cross. There is the cross itself, of course, and there are the crown of thorns, the scarlet cloak, the swords, the rod, the nails, and the rest. Each of these things—all of them long gone to dust, I suppose—bespeaks human violence and hostility: but also, in the context of this most special of stories, each of them also bespeaks the tenacious love of the God who is also a man, of a man who is also God. In the same spirit, let me point to two 'eloquent items'. They are, from near the beginning of the story, the aromatic spikenard ointment; and, from near the end, the vinegar on a sponge, held up to the crucified Christ.

One thing we can say for sure about the woman's pouring this luxurious and refreshing perfume over the Jesus eating dinner is that she did not have to do it. He could have got by without it: it had presumably never happened to him before, and never would again: he did not need it: nobody, in the strict sense, *needs* such a thing. But even as I say this I think of a great moment in Shakespeare's *King Lear* when that deprived king, being told that he doesn't actually need a retinue of followers, says, 'O reason not the need!.../Allow not nature more than nature needs,/ Man's life is cheap as beast's.' Lear's judgement about many things is astray, but this one he has right. In a sense we do need more than we 'need': we are hungry for the lavish; we yearn, and we were made to yearn, for amplitude, for prodigality. I think it was the American writer Eric Hoffer who said that nobody has ever been loved as we all long to be loved. He was wrong about the absence of the loving, but right about the presence of the longing. We are all after being loved extravagantly—being loved up to death and beyond—and we are insatiable until we are assured that the longing is vindicated.

The perfume poured over the Jesus who is, after all, there to get a meal he does need, stands for the divine lavishness which brought him, as a man, into being at all, as it brought you and me and all the world into being—and does so, each moment. It stands for the passionate enthusiasm of God our creator for each of us, and for us all. And at the same time it is the most appropriate of salutes to the Christ who is, himself, unstinting in his devotion both to that loving Father and to each of us. 'Sweets to the sweet' has sometimes been a saying: 'Lavishness to the lavish One' might be a saying for that moment.

And that is what sets the terms of reference for what we call the 'Passion' of our Lord. That 'Passion' is an undergoing, like the 'passion' of a patient in a hospital: but it is his passion for us, and for our good—for both our healing and our flourishing—that takes him into that undergoing. It is a bitter business, as the gospel reminds us, starkly. Near the end of it all, one of the execution squad holds up a spongeful of vinegar to him: and whether this is just another taunt, or is meant as some kind of relief, the bitterness of the stuff can remind us all of how actual, how immediate and unavoidable and invasive, all of the man's suffering is. We know, most of us, what it is to be hurt deeply, in body or in spirit or in both. When we think of that, we are thinking of the vinegary pain of Christ himself. It was real; it was his; and it killed him.

It would be fruitless, and it might be degraded, for us to think only of that pain—or in fact of any pain. It would also be selfish, and it might be callous, for us to turn abruptly from the suffering person. But unless, in thought and prayer, we confront the vinegar of suffering with the perfumed ointment of lavishness, not only are we missing the essential truth about God and about his living and loving Son Jesus, we are also giving the last word to that nexus of fear, hostility and calculation which got him into his lethal predicament at all.

Holy Week does, after all and true enough, appeal to us to be changed. It asks us not to stand to arms against one another, in thought, word or deed. It asks us to forego some at least of our resentments. It asks us to have a moratorium, if only for a few days, on the quarrel we are all inclined to have with God, who has had the bad taste to make us as we are and to give us what we have, and not arranged things otherwise. Holy Week, like all the other weeks, will bring us a ration of distresses, a reek of vinegar. But the worst vinegar of all, a self-administered vinegar, is to give up grateful hope in the God of the lavish. The poet Coleridge said that we should be 'obstinate in resurrection'; and whatever about poets, that is what God is.

*Newman: April, 2000*

# STORIES

## THE GOOD SAMARITAN

# *Good Samaritans*

15th Sunday in Ordinary time, Year C

OUR LORD'S PARABLE OF THE GOOD SAMARITAN has spoken to every age, and been spoken about in every age. In the last century, one wit said that there are plenty of people ready to do the good Samaritan without the oil or the twopence, which leaves, presumably, the pouring in of the wine. In our own century, the organization called 'Samaritans', in England, has saved many people from suicide. Recently, a book called *Bad Samaritans* criticized the giving of aid to stricken nations without doing anything about the system that is part of the strike against them. And this morning, like the rest of the Church throughout the world, we hear the parable told once more. What are we to make of it?

Each of us will have a personal way of hearing it; and if any story was ever meant to be taken personally, this is it. Each of us is far more mysteriously herself or himself than even the best of psychology or of sociology can bring out, since each of us is a unique expression of God's creative self; if we are tongue-tied when we try to utter our selfhood, that is partly because we are tongue-tied about God. But precisely because of the intimate connection between each of us and God, God's word can be our story. So a strong and tender tale like that of the good Samaritan can speak from the strength and tenderness of God into our own potential strength, our own potential tenderness. It can do so in one way, his way, to you: and in another way, which is also his way, to me. Let me tell you what it says to me today.

The Samaritan helped someone who was *in need*, and who was *different from himself*. The need is important. We often give things—not only physical things, but company, or advice, or support—to those who don't, strictly speaking, need these things. There is nothing wrong with that, and it can come from a certain lavishness of the heart in ourselves. Christianity actually encourages this, since at its centre is not mere survival but celebration, not mere good work but the generosity of grace. But giving into real need is different. It can put us in touch with our own fragility.

Visit someone seriously ill in hospital, and part of you is brought into contact with the mortality from which we all suffer. Give some hard-won knowledge into deep ignorance, and beside the consolation of seeing, sometimes, some improvement, there is likely to be an alertness to the radical ignorance about most things in life which is our common lot. The gift made into real need pulls the giver into insecurity, not clear of it. So the element of 'need' in the robbed and wounded Jew helped by the Samaritan is important.

And so is the fact that the Jew was *different*. Our Lord's clear, but disconcerting, message to us is that the fact that people are different from us does not license our ignoring them, or regarding them as expendable. Temperaments vary, I realize, and so do formative experiences in life: some people seem to have naturally hospitable hearts. It is a great gift of God's that they do. But it is probably not hard for most of us to acknowledge, at honest moments, that there are many who are, to us, deeply distasteful because of their 'otherness'.

In extreme cases, we might say that the world would be a better place without them. A Hitler, a Stalin, a Pol Pot: it is easy to see how one might hope and pray for their deaths. But to think much in those terms is, isn't it, to throw in one's lot to a degree with theirs; for these men are the monstrous haters of 'otherness'; they are the captives of the demon of narcissism. One would have to be very sure indeed, when making prayers about them, that one was not guided by the same spirit.

## Stories

In any case, we do not usually, at least consciously, think in such extreme terms. The needy 'others' in our lives may be pitched over the fence of our attention because they are, after all, of the wrong colour, or of the wrong—or indefinite—sex, or of the wrong political stripe, or are 'losers' on the one hand or 'silvertails' on the other. In Australia, angers can breed like rabbits, and we have fewer remedies against the angers than we have against the rabbits.

But everybody, without exception, in Australia has her or his own crucifixion—physical, social, moral, emotional, intellectual, or otherwise. Everybody bleeds, including those who most deny the fact, and including those who are most envied and hated by others because they seem to be denied the common human lot. Everybody will need a Samaritan one day. The poignancy of Jesus himself is that he needed one, at the end, and there was no human Samaritan to be had.

We may take hope, though, from our belief in the Lord's being raised up even out of the lethal wounding of death. He too, as the gospel says, 'fell among thieves'; he too was stripped of his clothes, and wounded until wounds could do no more. It is as if his Father then played the Samaritan to him, vitalizing him, and setting him on his way for all eternity. We are all, as Jesus himself was, stricken ones. Our lives have dealt us certain blows. The evolution of our species over hundreds of thousands of years has dealt us more blows still. Ourselves bruised, we are prone to bruise others; the Samaritan blood in us can run very thin.

Yet we come here today, you and I, in the hope that the Father who brought Jesus back from his stricken-ness may make bids for life in us too. We celebrate in this Mass the gift to us all of nothing less than the Spirit of Jesus, something better than the oil and the wine. Quite certainly, within the next few days, each of us will be given the opportunity to play the Samaritan, in little ways or great. Let us not be dispirited by past failures. It is the very meaning of the resurrection to give us a future—a future in which we may discover, in the place of some alien, a wounded sister, a wounded brother.

*Newman: July, 1992*

## THE PRODIGAL SON

## *Of Love and Waste*

24th Sunday in Ordinary Time, Year C

IN A WAY IT SEEMS BEST, AFTER WE HAVE HEARD the words of the story we call 'The Prodigal Son', to say nothing at all, and just let its majesty and tenderness take possession of us. But countless painters and poets have had something to say about it—and I hope that it has been set to music more than once—so perhaps I may go the way of my betters.

One thing to say about the story is that it is about love and waste. There is no doubt about the waste. The younger son, we are told, 'squandered his money on dissolute living'. He cannot escape this fact himself, and his older brother throws it in his face, and his father does not attempt to deny it. Waste is at the heart of the tale. But we would be sick of hearing about this if that were the last word. Rather, as Durer saw so clearly, and Rembrandt, and many others, the wastrel boy is gathered back into a milieu of love to which, as he knows, he has no title: and by this, we surely suppose, he is transformed.

Whatever you may say about the story, you cannot plausibly argue that it is out of date. Think, for a moment, about waste. The experience of having been a waster is one of the most durable of all experiences. Shakespeare's Richard II says at one point, 'I wasted time, and now doth time waste me', and one need not be a king, or even particularly old, to notice how, as we say, things catch up with us when, out of cowardice or avoidable foolishness or a policy of selfishness, we have lived trivially and kept ourselves morally and spiritually stunted. Jump several centuries, and you find that the most famous poem in English of the twentieth century is called 'The Waste Land', in which hearts and spirits are seen as burned-out for lack of proper care. Not only the hearts and spirits, either: the devastated cities, in peace or in war, bear the look they have not because of some uncontrollable natural force, but because of human carelessness, human selfishness, human cowardice. There are hundreds of entries on 'waste disposal' in the Yellow Pages, but none of them bears on this.

What does bear on it? Well, up to a point, there are the things which most of us were probably told when we were very small. If our parents were not outright fools, they must have told us that wasting food or money or time was not a good policy. They were right then, and they would be right now. But unless we in our turn are outright fools, we also know that none of us has herself or himself perfectly in hand, and that the best advice in the world cannot of itself always deliver the goods. Our integrity and our wisdom can be sapped by unruly desires, by irresponsible friends and companions, by competitiveness, by laziness. There is a prodigal son, or a prodigal daughter, nesting in the heart of each of us, and it is easy enough, sometimes, to let them have their own perverse way. The road to the waste land is not necessarily glamorous or enchanting: we can still get there by seedy little by-paths.

Usually, what does bring us back to less futile or wasteful kinds of living is in fact the sway of love. It may need to be robust love, or stern love—only God can tell what is in fact called for—or it may dawn upon us that we are surrounded by such evidences of loving care that we had best change our ways somewhat in order to live in that real world, rather than in delusory zones of fear, aggression, and narcissism. When we do identify some people as rich in love, one of the things we may see in them is that they seem both full and focussed as human beings: evidently, they are not going to waste. And when, from prayer, or from someone's generosity to us, or by some other means, we are won back again and again to believe in the force of love in the world, this too is a way of our own living fruitfully.

Bread for the Journey

There are plenty of things in our Australian environment, and in the environment of the world as a whole, which press against this growth in us. Resentment and cynicism are two of the most damaging of forces. The elder son in our Lord's story is both resentful and cynical. He resents his father's lavishness to the brother who is admittedly a wastrel, and he is cynical about any good outcome from that lavishness. Indeed, his voice may be said to be the voice of the devil—scornful, dismissive, in love with futility. It is a voice easy to hear in Australia, and not only in the mouths of demagogues. The diabolic voice, bitter, belittling, and self-shielding, can be heard in any pub, on any campus, and in any university college.

But even when that happens, the whole logic of today's parable is that we should not despair either of ourselves or of one another. Contempt for other people, contempt for ourselves, is the ultimate waste: but from that, too, we can be drawn back. The despised Christ descended into the pit of whatever is contemptible in us, and in his rising draws us with love's unkillable force. This Mass, like all of them is an act of gratitude, an act of thanksgiving: and that rising, that raising, is the major thing for which we are grateful.

*Newman: September, 1998*

JOHN THE
BAPTIST

## Taking Away the Sins of the World

2nd Sunday in Ordinary Time, Year A

IF YOU WERE TO RUMMAGE THROUGH ANY sizeable illustrated history of the visual arts of the Western world, you would come across some portrayals of John the Baptist—John the Baptizer, as some call him. He makes a good subject for a painter who wants things to be vivid and dramatic. There he is, scraggy, solitary, looming out of the desert—a bit dirty, more than a bit awkward, red-eyed, noisy, intractable: a prophet's prophet, in fact; barely house-broken, and if not a breaker-in of houses, at least a hammerer-away at hearts. He has been carved, and printed, and painted, times without number.

Today's Gospel records this weird figure as saying of his cousin, Jesus, 'Look—there is the Lamb of God, who takes away the sin of the world'. It is ancient talk, and if we were to take it in isolation it might strike us as bizarre. We do not, nowadays, attempt to court God through ritual sacrifice: I dare say that nobody here today has ever cut the throat of a lamb in the hope that things would, as a result, go better for her, or for him. So the talk about Jesus as sacrificed lamb is likely to remain, for most of us, imaginatively odd, and culturally remote.

What is not odd or remote, though, is the fact that the bulk of individual lives—yours perhaps, mine perhaps—can be devoted to a largely-selfless service of other people. We pour time and energies into policies which we would not, ideally, have chosen for ourselves: and sometimes that 'pouring' takes up the best hours or years of our lives. Any one of us who has been half-way decent knows something about sacrifice, whether or not we called it that at an earlier time.

So far so good: but what the lean, mean man from the desert says, directly or indirectly, is not only that we are all summoned to live generously, but that the arrival of Jesus is the arrival of the one who 'takes away the sin of the world'. What does this mean? And how can it be so? Well, whatever it means, it means more than what was talked about officially in the Soviet Union after Stalin was safely dead.

Some of us will remember that, after all the adulation of that monster, the Communist Party of the Soviet Union eventually got around to acknowledging that Stalin had committed various 'mistakes'. 'Mistakes' was the way in which a reign of terror and the murder of tens of millions of people were talked about. When we say that Jesus, Son of God, takes away the sin of the world, we are not talking only about his rectifying certain blunders, his re-adjusting the moral order of the world as though it were an old clock prone to run too fast or too slow. We are talking about his putting himself in the thick of outrageous evil, and his allowing that outrageous evil to impinge upon him to the death-point, and his conquering death *and sin* by such a love for us, and a love for his Father, that the vileness of evil is denied the last word, and the world is saved, as we say, 'for good'.

I suppose that, in order to have some inkling as to how this comes about, we would need to be, not great theologians, but common or garden saints. And since, by God's grace, there are streaks of sanctity, broad or narrow streaks, in all of us, we do have some such inkling. We know, when we let it come home to us, that the patient tenderness of mothers is a retort, of sorts, to the selfishness which so easily taints their children's lives. We know that honest, creditable work of the mind or the body, can hearten us and give us vitality of spirit, in the face of cynical and trashy behaviour. We know that every human generation has some of its sense of direction, some of its morale, some of its soundness, because generations before it have made provision for it. The roof stays on this chapel, the candles burn as they should, even our clothes fit us, because people have passed on competencies down the centuries—and have done so not only for the sake of money or of praise, but because it was good that they should do so.

These pieces of behaviour, you may say, are commonplace, and they certainly bear no specifically religious marking. This is true: but then, that is just the way the dear Lord goes on working out in time the salvation he brings us, the taking away of the sin of the world. Our sins—yours, mine, the world's at large—have something of what Hannah Arendt once called 'the banality of evil': we let one another down in predictable, all-too-familiar ways; and we give up on ourselves, and to a degree on God, in the dull modes of laziness and greed and the gradual callousings of the heart. And by the same token, it is into our common days—not only the red-letter days of Sunday, or of Australia Day, or of Christmas Day, but the black-letter days of any calendar—that the saving love of God inserts itself—or, since that saving love is indeed the Holy Spirit, inserts himself, or herself.

And so, to come back to John the Baptist, we do well to follow his injunction, when he says, 'Look—there is the Lamb of God, who takes away the sin of the world'. God's sacrificial love is there to be seen, all about us, if only our eyes are opened. At this Mass, in the first month of a new year, let us pray for one another that we will indeed see what is to be seen: that in a wounded world, the Healer and the Life-Giver is at work, incessantly.

*Newman: January, 1996*

THE LORD'S
PRAYER

# *Our Father*

### 17th Sunday in Ordinary time, Year C

JUST BEFORE WE COME TO THE COMMUNION RITE in this Mass, I will say, 'Jesus taught us to call God our Father, and so we have the courage to say, "Our Father ..."'. And if we have the courage to say the Our Father, perhaps I can have to courage to say a few words about that best of prayers.

The first words of this prayer are perhaps the most important. For many people they may also be the most improbable, the hardest to believe. For they claim, don't they, that the ultimate truth about this world, and any possible world, is that it is held in fatherly care. We may find this a hard saying for either of two reasons. The first is simply that the whole thing is simply so big, and so intricate. I don't need to give you a recitative of figures about galaxies, their age and their distance: we have all heard them before, and unless we are professionally concerned with them, they tend to slide off the mind like food off Teflon. But if we do find ourselves up some modest-sized mountain, or on water out of sight of land, or even in the thick of a decently large city, we may be struck by the muchness of it all, its anonymity, and its indifference to our presence. Any attempt to actually picture a personal being presiding over all this can come to feel more like cartoon-behaviour than anything else: whatever we can do with the gigantic, we can't feel at home with it.

And the other problem with claiming God as Father of it all is of course the presence of everything that grieves and dispirits us,

212

everything that outrages us. How can it be fatherly behaviour that we should have to live mortally—so briefly, often so ineptly and sometimes so badly—and this in a world so given to natural disaster and human shamefulness?

Human beings, Christians among them, have wrestled with these questions for about as long as they have been writing things down, and presumably for much longer than that. I am not offering answers here, if indeed they are to be had. I simply want to point out that when we begin to say the 'Our Father,' as adults, we are in effect giving the lie to our own scepticism, and the scepticism of others. We are, implicitly, asking for help in dismissing the old, cold voice that says that we are without help. We are not being polite to God in saying 'Our Father': we are asking him to win us back to the genuine trust of children who are in good circumstances. Early in the testing of the first atomic bombs, after one such test, one official turned to another and said, 'Now we are all bastards.' Saying the 'Our Father' is an acknowledgement that God will not view us as bastards, whatever we do, and whatever comes our way. On the contrary.

The other thing I want to say about this prayer is that our calling God our Father the 'Holy' one is very important. 'Holiness' is a term which can leave us quite unmoved, or, if moved, merely uncomfortable. An old Irish priest said once of somebody, 'He's a holy man—and a good man, too,' which catches the reservation we can feel about holiness as aloofness, or holiness as otherworldly. But one way of thinking of God as holy is to think of him as the untainted one. We are tainted by our own moral lacks and refusals to grow, and we can be tainted by our milieu. Very easily, even in frequently-kindly Australia, we can be tainted by our cynicisms, our scornings, our indulged darknesses of spirit. When we say that God is holy, is 'hallowed', we say among other things that he is not like this at all. He is a holy God, and a good God too. He is utterly without illusion, but utterly given to loving. He is the first good thing, and the last good thing, the best thing of all for each of us. It is an excellent state of affairs that we are told to dare to call him 'Our Father'.

*Newman: July, 1998*

ZACCHAEUS

## *Outsiders*
### 31st Sunday in Ordinary Time, Year C

IF YOU GO INTO ANY SIZEABLE BOOKSHOP THESE days you can get hold of a book published not so long ago. It is the paperback edition of Albert Camus' *The First Man*, the manuscript of which was with him in the car-crash which killed him. For various reasons, it had to wait thirty-five years before being published, but now that it is out Camus' name has become prominent again. Whatever you may think of *The First Man*, its author will surely be remembered most of all for his first novel, *L'Etranger*, known variously in English as *The Stranger* or *The Outsider*.

In that book, its protagonist is, from first to last, an outsider indeed. He lives as one and he dies as one. And consider the titles of some of Camus' other books: *The Plague, The Rebel, The Myth of Sisyphus, The Fall, Exile and the Kingdom, Caligula and Three Other Plays, The Possessed, Resistance, Rebellion and Death*. They all sound as if they are, as indeed they are, about the condition of being an outsider.

I mention all this because what we have in today's Gospel is the spectacle of an outsider's being made an insider, by the grace of God in Jesus. The commentators point out that Zacchaeus' name means 'the innocent or righteous one', but that is not the way he is seen by some at least of his fellow citizens. It is probably hard for most of the citizenry to warm to the collectors of taxation—whose heart goes out to the men and women in grey who check the parking meters? And if we remember that

Israel was an occupied country, and that some taxes went to Roman authorities or to those operating concessions under them, it is not hard to see how someone like Zacchaeus could be regarded as 'not quite the thing,' to put it mildly. His critics at least think of him as tainted, as having some of the reek of the rotten about him.

He is in short an outsider. And when the little man gets himself up into a tree in order to see Jesus amidst the crowd, he is not up some byword for grace like a palm tree, he is up the stubby sycamore tree; he is physically an outsider as well as socially. But then, as the Gospel tells us, he is called down from his perch by Jesus, who says that he has to go and be a house-guest of Zacchaeus'. So down he comes, and in they go, and Jesus endorses him, and Zacchaeus gives half his goods to the poor and says that if he happens to have treated anybody unjustly, he will make it up, with damages thrown in.

A story with a happy ending, in short, though it would not have made our Lord any the more popular with his ingrained critics, part of whose agenda was to keep the wall between insiders and outsiders too high for anyone to get over, however tall his tree. When we think of what this word of God's may have to say to us this evening, I am reminded again of Camus, who thought at two levels. An Algerian himself, he knew what it was to be socially on the margin of things, and he found out in the bitter mid-century years what it was to be living in Occupied France, and after that what it was to be a man of the Left but anti-Stalinist in French intellectual circles. He looked start-lingly like Humphrey Bogart, and used to keep a Bogart poster on his wall, and there was in his real life something of the doomed outsider type often played by Bogart. It got him a following, but it also got him bitter hostility. That is one level, the social.

The other level is the philosophical, the elemental. Camus' profoundest concern was not with whether, for instance, Sartre or Simone de Beauvoir or Arthur Koestler was right about politics, but with where we are in existence itself. Are we outsiders after all, perpetually marginalized from love and meaning, random organisms in a chilling cosmos? Is there a home to take us in, body and soul, so that we may like Jesus and Zacchaeus face one another across a festal

'... its protagonist is, from first to last, an outsider indeed. He lives as one and dies as one.'

table, and be at home indeed? Camus thought not: but in all his abbreviated life, he never stopped thinking about it.

I suppose, my brothers and sisters, that none of us would be here this evening if we thought, like Camus, that we are finally bereft. Already in this Eucharist we have affirmed our belief in a God of blessings, and we have gloried, briefly, in his love of us, and we have just heard words which help to fortify our God-given conviction. And as the Mass unfolds, we will in effect make ourselves still more at home in this house of God, as we listen once more to the story of his loving deeds in the past and his promises for our future, and then take from his table divine food for our human needs. These are not the actions of outsiders.

But it is the common tradition of the Church that those of its community, its household, cannot be authentically Christian unless they turn their faces towards the others in need. These days, the word 'solidarity' is often used in Christian parlance, though some of us learned it not from any Christian quarter but from Camus: either way, the fact remains that we cannot be Christian insiders unless, like Jesus, we feel the imperative tug of outsiders in their need.

Those needy ones may show themselves to us mainly at the social level. As we all know, at this moment, there are millions of refugee outsiders in the world, bereft of homes, and often bereft of hope. Apart from them, there are the less dramatically visible but still chronically needy ones of our own Melbournian neighbourhood. Some of them have no equivalent of a sycamore tree into which they can hoist themselves and be noticed: but there they are, and their social invisibility is itself another of their pains. 'As you did to one of these my least ones, so you did to me': we hope one day to hear these words said to us by the unillusioned Lord, that day when how things truly stand in the world will be seen for the first time. God grant that we may have more to point to than benign sentiments and good wishes: for we shall be speaking to a scarred Jesus.

But there is also need of another sort, the ontological or existential need, which is expressed in intellectual or imaginative forms, but is as truly of the heart and soul as any other kind of need. This is the need for meaning, the need not to be meaningless. If it turns out, for an individual or for a society, there is a void at the heart of existence—not hostility, not benignity, just nothing—then the doom of the outsider re-asserts itself. Presumably we all know that just such a view is the central philosophical tenet (if such it can be called) of post-modernity: that when you take the lid off what is labelled 'society' or 'human personality', you find that there is nothing inside; and there is certainly no divine agent to put something under the lid.

Frankly, I find this a diabolic teaching in the strict sense: it is the work of the devil. But even if you take a more sanguine view of it, you will surely grant that Australian society needs and deserves as well-informed and deeply-considered an understanding of what on earth human life is about as it can get. The less we do believe that everyone, man woman or child, is one of God's insiders, the readier we may be to kill them off at the beginning or the end of their lives: and God alone knows what we will do with people for the rest of their lives. Things like this have to be thought about, and then something done about the thoughts.

These days, it would be naive to expect secular universities to do much of the leg-work for us, for they are often part of the problem; and anyone who thinks that salvation comes from Spring Street or from Canberra must have dozed off for a while. By contrast, places like Newman College, or St Mary's College, or Mannix College, exist in the hope of fostering a Christian agenda—an agenda which, without any kind of triumphalism, can genuinely be of service, sometimes confronting service, to God's meaning-seeking, meaning-needing children.

It is not much fun, being an outsider, however many distractions one may have. In Argentina, the figure of the gaucho is often romanticized, the gaucho who is solitary, hard-riding, out there beyond the margins. It can sound good: but the word 'gaucho' means 'fatherless, orphaned, illegitimate', and if there is a legend that gauchos start singing in their mother's wombs, they are always singing about trouble.

You don't see gauchos in Swanston Street, or in Collins Street: but there are plenty of exiled, outsider spirits, however fine their clothing. Let us pray in this Mass for a heightened sense of the Lord's making a home with us, and a home for us: and let us pray to face his other children with eyes and a heart like his.

*Newman: November, 1995 (Mass for Founders & Benefactors)*

THE
CANAANITE
WOMAN

## *Providence and Pressure*

### 20th Sunday in Ordinary Time, Year A

I BEGIN THESE FEW WORDS BY COMING CLEAN WITH you: if you do not think that you are under any pressure in life, nor expect to be under pressure, this is a good moment to switch off for a while, until the Creed and the Prayers of the Faithful and, of course, the collection. But, for anyone else who may now still be listening—let us consider what has happened in the Gospel passage we have just heard.

It is in fact all about *people under pressure*. The basic problem is that the daughter of a woman from Canaan is, as the mother says, 'terribly troubled by a demon'. None of us knows what this meant in the particular case, except that it made for (as we say) a hell of a lot of anxiety. The daughter's situation may have been physical, or psychological, or spiritual, but whatever it was, it was a long way away from serenity—the young woman was being, somehow, savaged. And the pressure she was under put her mother under pressure.

I don't need to dwell on this. It's no easy ride bearing a child even in the skilled, rich Western world in the late twentieth century, and it never has been in the past: and when, at a cost, one has that replica of oneself, a daughter, for her to be savaged is a drastic thing.

Distress radiates: distress diffuses itself. The woman from Canaan, grabbing at any chance she has, appeals to the passing Christ, who, she believes, has something to offer. When she gets no immediate satisfaction from him, she does what any of us would do—she goes to his assistants, or minders: she goes to the disciples. So he, Jesus, is under pressure, and so, as they quickly tell him, are they: they urge him to do something about her, in order to get her off their backs.

God knows what the disciples said to her. Perhaps they said that things would improve, or that she should go to the back of the queue, or something of the sort. There is a bitter old Irish saying which goes, 'It's easy to lie on another man's wound,' meaning that our aches are our own and other people adjust to them quickly enough. But she was louder than their business, or tiredness, or indifference: she was in effect making *her* wound *theirs*, so that they couldn't lie on it so easily after all.

But the eerie, the almost creepy, case is that of her dealings with Jesus. She gets beyond the social barriers and talks to him, and it certainly sounds, first up, as if he has nothing to offer the likes of her. He too, after all, is under pressure. He is only one man, and whether or not he knows that he has not long to live, he can't be expected to cope with everybody. He sees himself as called to be there for his own ethnic and cultural and religious group, as pretty well any of us would. God knows, being under Roman occupation as they are, the whole lot of them need all the concentrated help they can get. To be under long-standing military occupation messes a people about very badly, as the twentieth century can teach us; and this lot, when enthusiasts had run riot years ago, had seen the sky darkened with crucified bodies.

So Jesus tells her to get lost. He doesn't say that Peter will take her name and address, or that James or John will look into the matter at some appropriate time. He tells her to get lost. To which she says that, even if she is a reject, rejects too have a right to some hearing and some help. To which he says that he can't argue against that, and so he heals her daughter. End of story.

If that were really the end of the story, we would not be listening to it this morning. Because Christianity is not all about the telling of charming stories, and the listening to them. If it were, it would indeed be infantile, as many suppose it is; and I have better things to do with my life than just to be telling nice little stories to even the nicest of people. No, the fact is that the word of God is like the match with which I lit the candles on the altar here, a little while ago. Something is supposed to happen to us when we are touched by it. Some of our stiff indifference is supposed to be touched, as happened when the flame got at the beeswax. Some of our dark, still, inward being is meant, like the wick, to catch fire.

If that happens, this time round, what may result? Perhaps this. I may begin to see that the tide of divine love can lift to meet me *even when I am under pressure*. If ever teachers of spirituality, or exhorters to moral excellence, said that what we had to do to lift our moral game was to get free of pressures, they were being extremely stupid. I'm not sure whether that's what they ever were saying, but if it was, that's what they were.

The Father of heaven and earth, and Jesus Christ his Son, and the enchanted and enchanting Spirit of them both, play their love forth to us in the midst of pressures, many of which we did not choose, and all of which we have to cope with. Think of our crucifix. Amongst the many things that can be said about it, one is that it is a place where tensions meet: another is that the living God, a living man, is right there: and a third is that from the heart of those pressures, from that knotted tree, our hope of eternal love blossoms.

Hundreds of years ago, in 1453, the first printed Bible came out. It was, physically, the word of God 'under pressure': it was produced by what we now call 'the Press'. The technology has changed since then, and the word of God has reverberated in areas of which Gutenberg, the printer, knew nothing—not least, in Australia.

But the word of God is always under the pressure of cynicism and of scepticism, since many of us find its combination of love and challenge hard to take. Still, one thing our gospel passage today puts squarely before us is the claim that *where we are pressed, there we can be met*. It is in stress, too, that we intersect with God.

*Newman: August, 1996*

ABRAHAM

# *The Abraham Within*
## 2nd Sunday of Lent, Year A

IF, DURING OFFICE HOURS, YOU GO OVER TO THE Baillieu Library at the University of Melbourne, and speak to them nicely, someone will take you into the Special Collection of books and let you look at facsimile reproductions of medieval volumes in which various passages from the Bible are illustrated—or, as we say, illuminated: the light seems to shine out of them. It does this almost literally, because of the brilliancy of decoration—with the reds and blues and sundry other colours, and above all, the golds. What has happened here is that various words or phrases have seized the imaginations, have printed themselves on the souls, of readers all those hundreds of years ago, and they in turn have high-lighted these. The Bible is not just a Bible-at-large: it is *somebody's* Bible, made memorable with a view to what those readers found precious.

The habit has not died out, of course: you may have done your own underlining, or high-lighting; certainly, at least one edition of the Bible I can think of puts some things in big print and some in smaller, to meet the enthusiasms of one particular editor. And historically, one way of handling the whole Bible, Old and New Testaments, has been to put today's first reading, about Abraham's call, right at the beginning of the whole thing—before the Flood, before the Garden of Eden, before the Creation: up front, there are the words, 'The Lord said to Abram, "Leave your country, your family and your father's house, for the land I will show you'". I suggest to you today that we would do well, at least for a while, to do the same thing.

Why should this be? Above all, it is because, as our individual lives unfold, and as our shared lives unfold, the same summons goes on being made to us. Time after time, we are called to leave behind good and familiar things, and to step forward into what (so God says) will be good, but which is certainly unfamiliar. For some of us this may be—for some of us it may already have been—the stepping, or sailing, or flying, or fleeing, from one literal country, family, and traditional home, and the gradual insertion into another country, family, and home. For some of us it may be more modest, but still significant; we stay within the same broad contours on the map, but we make a new life, if we can, within a fresh configuration of acquaintances, friends, challengers.

Either way, the demands can be considerable, and we can lose heart—not necessarily altogether lose heart, but to such an extent that we scale down hopes, scale down expectations. Now God knows that God does not expect us to live in starry-eyed fashion; we have to be taught by experience, even if some of its lessons are bitter ones. But it seems to me that the whole brunt, the whole thrust, of both the Old and the New Testaments is that we should be very slow indeed to concede the last word to bitter experiences.

Anyone who is, outright, of that disposition, should logically get up and leave this Mass right now: because the bitter, crucified condition of our Lord is not only held up to us in the form of the crucifix, but is named explicitly as we proceed. It is only because we always insist on naming his being raised from that vile, unjust death, that we can come after all to Communion. And apart from anything else, this presses us to consider how, in our personal distresses or in the distresses of a gravely suffering world, we may hope after all to trace some retrieval, some creativity, some transformation. The biblical saying, 'Leave your country', can refer not only to geographical manoeuvers, but to the closed country of disappointments, of burned fingers, of partly atrophied hearts.

But there is another point I would make, simpler than this first one, so simple as perhaps to be over-obvious. It is that, every day to some extent, and every year inescapably, we are called out of the country of experience which we have been inhabiting, into unknown terrain. It you look around in the larger bookshops, you will find plenty of books which are concerned with 'stages on life's journey'— with childhood and adolescence and young adulthood and middle age and all the rest of it. The more of these the better, I think: but a moment's reflection will tell us that the books cannot take the place of the thing itself. Having come to deal, more or less competently, with the business of being in one's twenties, all of a sudden it seems that the forties are here—and what happened to the thirties—not to speak of later stretches? I really do believe that, for a lot of people, much of their deepest moral identity, much of the context of their growing or withering spiritually, is in the attitude they take to the fact that, so to speak, life's rug is in time pulled out from each of us. Do we then believe, can we then believe, that we are being called into a new country which God, the maker of countries, is offering to us?

I am not only talking about heaven, here, even though, apart from God himself, there is probably nothing I believe in so much as heaven. I am talking about a readiness to reverence, and cherish, and foster, the lives we palpably have and palpably share: and to do this in spite of disappointment and disillusionment and outright surprise. When God is finishing his call to Abraham, he says that 'all the communities of the earth shall find blessing in you'. There is, in effect, an Abraham within each of us, an Abraham of the heart, who is being called, day by day, towards creativity. The best next step any of us can take is to affirm, in faith and hope, that that is so.

*Newman: March, 1996*

SHEPHERDS

## *Like Sheep*
11th Sunday of Ordinary Time, Year A

I HAVE A BRIEF WORD TO SAY, NOW, ABOUT shepherds. Some of us may have been shepherds: all of us will have seen versions of them in Christmas cribs and in various Christian paintings. In a rough and ready way, we know what they do—as they have been doing for thousands of years, in many parts of the world.

We also know that our Lord spoke of himself as a good shepherd—in fact, as the best of shepherds. It was natural for him to do this, living as he did in a largely rural community. It was also a traditional sort of a thing to do, since one of the best-remembered of culture-heroes in Israel was the great king David, who started out as a shepherd, and whose leadership while a king was sometimes conceived of as a kind of shepherding. And there is another note to our Lord's adopting the style of 'shepherd', since it had become customary to call God Himself the 'shepherd of Israel'. This flesh-and-blood good shepherd was linking himself with the Great Shepherd of all the world.

I am mentioning these things because, in the Gospel passage today, it is said that Jesus finds his heart going out in compassion to his people because they were 'harassed and dejected, like sheep without a shepherd'. Essentially, our own situation is no different. I don't mean that we all feel harassed and dejected all the time—obviously we don't, and thank God for that. What I do mean is that, so long as we live, we all need a kind of shepherding. We need it as individuals, and we need it as groups. And when we sense that we are not getting it, things can go badly wrong.

In less than two years we will have done with this century as a set of dates, but many people will not, so long as they live, have done with it as a predicament, or milieu, or web of influences. Infamously, at the very least, scores of millions of people have died wretchedly because they found themselves under the sway of bogus shepherds. Hitler was called, in German, 'the leader': Mussolini was called, in Italian, 'the leader': Stalin was called by hordes of titles, but they all amounted to 'the leader': and so was Mao: and so were a long tally of other enemies of humanity—as some indeed still are. All of these figures were, not wolves in sheep's clothing, but wolves in shepherds' clothing. And they were deathly beings: they were of the devil.

To many of us they are mere names, or mere cartoon-figures. But we should not, too easily, forget about them, since none of them would have been possible if there were not, indeed, a deep human hunger to be shepherded. That hunger is God-given, and it can be God-satisfied: but it can also be abused. There is nobody in this chapel today who could have learned to walk or to talk without having been shepherded into these things: and to get closer to our situation, neither a university nor a university college has any credible rationale except with a view to shepherding and to benefiting from that shepherding. But in a fallen world, there is no such thing as untainted shepherding, unambiguous shepherding—as we may see, not only within universities and university colleges, but even within that continued expression of the Good Shepherd, the Church.

My real word to you today, then, is this: if you suppose that nobody, or nothing, is shepherding you right now, you are certainly wrong. You have, as I have, good shepherds and bad shepherds. The good shepherds (who are themselves animated by the Holy Spirit of the Good Shepherd) are helping you to flourish in generosity, in bravery, in alertness to God's new moves in a constantly renewed world. The bad shepherds—and you can find their imprint any time you flick from one channel to another on TV, or surf the Web, or listen for a while in a pub or a bus or a supermarket—the bad shepherds will be pandering to your narcissism, to your timidity, to your indulged angers, to your greed, to your cherished contempts.

The need to discern, to divine, to discriminate, between the good shepherds and the bad ones will be with you as long as you are a responsible human being. This is good news, though demanding—no mere sheep, after all, could do it. It presumes that we have both minds and hearts: and it presumes that we have the great Good Shepherd on our side. But it also presumes that when men and women desert discernment, when they become the playthings of spurious shepherds, things can go wrong again and again. Even one Hitler was one too many.

*Newman: June, 1999*

## JESUS' GENEROSITY

# *Gambles*

### 22nd Sunday in Ordinary Time, Year A

SOME OF YOU MAY REMEMBER A MOMENT IN Robert Bolt's play, *A Man for All Seasons*, or the film made from it, at which Sir—later Saint—Thomas More is on trial, and is lyingly accused by a former servant of official corruption. More notices that the man is wearing some insignia, and asks what it is. He is told that his denouncer (whose name, ironically, is 'Richard Rich') is, in effect, now running Wales. And to this More says, 'What does it profit a man to gain the whole world, and suffer the loss of his own soul? But for *Wales*, Richard— for *Wales*!'

It is gallant, and British, and snobbish: and it is right. Anything would be a bad bargain at the Last Day, as More knows, if one has sold one's integrity for it. Thomas More, by contrast, is on trial at all simply because he has not been prepared to cut such a deal. He does not want to be a hero, and he certainly does not want to die. He argues with all the skills of a great lawyer and of one of the geniuses of the English Renaissance; he comes on as strong as a figure in Shakespeare might. But at the end, he will not buy space, as Rich buys Wales, and he will not buy time, if that is tainted time. He declines to put his very soul, his very self, on the gambling-table of sheer pragmatism. He wants to have something left, wants to have some*one* left, for the green land and sunshine of eternity.

More probably got such notions from classical and biblical models, the heroes and heroines of integrity who had bolstered many before him, and who bolster some to this day. But essentially he got the message from our Lord Jesus, and most of all no doubt from the passage we have heard in the Gospel today, where that Lord Jesus challenges us about our ultimate values, before going to put that challenge to the test of his own betrayal, his own execution.

I think that we should remember how un-fanatical, how companionable and 'normal,' our Lord is in many episodes in the gospels. The crowds who follow him could survive without a meal's being laid on; it would not hurt them much to go home hungry: but he feeds them. The people at the wedding reception of Cana may, for all I know, be running short of wine because they have been drinking harder than is good for them—but anyway, high-quality wine is what they get: they start off with Jacob's Creek, and they wind up with Grange Hermitage. A long-crippled man, met on the sabbath, could have hung on for another, less-contentious day, to be healed: but no, here and now is where he is, so here and now is where he is healed. Various aliens complicate the already-demanding life of the wandering preacher and challenger—an interloping Roman officer wants help for one of his servants; a Samaritan woman won't even give him a drink of water without a theological argument; the Canaanite woman of whom we heard recently keeps at him, and at him, with the humiliating wailing of the desperate. He responds to each of these; and even if, as is appropriate, the Church has over the centuries read more general, edifying lessons out of these ad-hoc pieces of down-to-earth generosity, those lessons would have no bite or plausibility at all unless Jesus the Short-Lived had really been responding to his fellow short-lived human beings, as someone in need to others in need.

I am saying that he was sensible. That isn't everything in a woman or a man, but finally nothing much about a woman's or a man's claims has much credibility if they are *not* sensible. Yet it is just this sensible, down-to-earth man who goes on confronting me, and confronting you, as to how we are investing our energies, our allegiances, our passions, our skills, our time—in a word, ourselves. He knows now, as he knew then, that there is a good deal of lee-way in life, often enough: that we try things on for size, that we punt on this chance or that, just as we may punt on the stock market, or on various forms of insurance. All of that is tolerable, and some of it is necessary; life is, up to a point, a wheel of fortune. Nobody, not even Jesus, has ever been a supreme commander in life.

But to take some chances is madness. It can never be an act of sanity to play Russian roulette. And that, in effect, is what our Gospel passage is talking about today—playing Russian roulette. Because to play fast and loose with our integrity, whether at some drastic moment, or through some long, slow process, is something for which there is no human remedy. Nobody will give us Wales for it, these days: nobody will give us anything that lasts, at all.

*Newman: September, 1996*

THE NEW ADAM

# *If I Am the One, Let These Others Go*
## Good Friday, Year B

WHEN WE READ OR HEAR THIS PASSION STORY, it is easy I think for us to feel numbed. This is partly because of the horror of it all, and partly because we know it so well, and partly because we find its elements being re-enacted, century after century and also week after week. It may be appropriate, in fact, for us not to reach too quickly, of a Good Friday, for lucid, emphatic feeling; the numbness may be the right thing in the face of what we know.

Even so, our attention may still be caught afresh by one detail or another in the narrative—as mine is by our Lord's words, 'If I am the one you are looking for, let these others go.' Perhaps this is no 'detail' after all: perhaps it points to the whole meaning of the Lord's Passion, insofar as we can understand it. For one of the central, traditional christian teachings is, as we say in the Creed, that it is for us, and for our salvation, that God's Son becomes our brother: he makes our sake his own sake, through and through.

In a famous formulation, the German theologian Dietrich Bonhoeffer called Christ the 'man for others'. Bonhoeffer had, so to speak, a special right to use that phrase, since, when he was safe in America from the attentions of Hitler, he still decided to return to Germany to continue the theological and spiritual service of his people and to resist the Nazis: in the event, he was executed as a result. Bonhoeffer too was a 'man for others': but, good and heroic man though he was, he could not be a 'God for others'. A sinner and a mortal like the rest of us, he could not stand, definitively and intimately, at the heart of another's human need, or at the heart of the world's universal need, and keep faith with it lovingly to the end. And that is what our Lord did, and does, 'for us, and for our salvation'.

'If I am the one you are looking for, let these others go.' I think that these words signal to us two things—integrity, and compassion. The two do not always go together conspicuously in human behaviour. There are some people of integrity—of moral coherence—who at least seem relatively indifferent to others and their condition: they may indeed be heroic in a sense, but they are somewhere else from the rest of us, and they do not seem to be 'for' us: they are 'for' something. On the other hand, there are people who do genuinely warm to the need of others, and who labour on their behalf, but who seem somewhat centre-less themselves: it is as if they have functions rather than a core.

Our Lord did not come to be, as it were, a moral 'star', a triumphant ethical and human performer: for him to be thought of as giving 'the Jesus Christ show' would have seemed to him absurd and abhorrent. But it is certainly true that our species, our human community, our world, is saved from hellish futility, and saved for splendid vitality, only because integrity and compassion are fused in this one man, God's Son.

As to the integrity, we remember that Jesus is called the 'New Adam', a fresh start for us all. The first Adam, challenged by God as to his wrong-doing, says in effect, 'It wasn't my fault, it was Eve's fault'. He tries to take himself out of the dock, tries to disappear from sight. By contrast, our Lord, at that moment of betrayal and seizure, does not attempt to melt away, nor to shield himself behind others, but is prepared to be accosted in the middle of the mess.

He is not guilty: he will say repeatedly, and to different authorities, that he is innocent, and that they have no right to touch him, let alone to punish him. He is, as we say, his own man, and by contrast with Adam he is a free man. The poet and exile Joseph Brodsky said once that being free means that you have no one to blame: our Lord does not get into the blaming business, any more than into the shielding business. But he is very clear on the fact—how could he not be?—that the whole situation is a dreadful mess. It reeks of feebleness, and viciousness, and pitilessness, and lies. It is enough to make anyone despair of human beings: but he cannot do this—it is for their sake that he has come—and he does not do this. No buck gets passed, no pawn gets sacrificed—not by him. He is the buck, he is the pawn: and he is the only completely sound human being there.

St John tells us, in the Gospel we have just heard, that when our Lord says, 'If I am the one you are looking for, let these others go', he is living out the truth of what he had said previously—'I have not lost a single one of those you [my Father] entrusted to me.' In the end, those entrusted to Jesus are not only the few with whom he has just shared a last meal, but all men and women, without qualification and without distinction. Judas is entrusted to him, and Caiaphas, and Pilate, and the execution squad, and his mother, and the bandits crucified next to him, and you, and I, and Saddam Hussein, and Australia's worst drug-dealer, and everybody else. It is to the cross of compassion for each of these, for each of us, that Jesus will be fixed. This the Lord in whose name, and by whose example, we will pray for a world in need. Let us pray, too, that he will open the heart of each of us: and let us pray that he will put heart into all of us.

*Newman: April, 2000*

# CREED

THE NICENE
CREED

## *We Believe ...*

A USUAL THING TO DO AT THIS TIME OF THE Homily is for the celebrant to reflect on the readings of the day, and this is what I usually do. But there are other possibilities; and one of them is to reflect on some other part of the Mass. It occurs to me that, on every Sunday of the year, we say the Creed together—as indeed we will say it today. And since the Creed is a crystallization of what is crucial to our beliefs as Christians, I propose, sometimes, to offer some thoughts about it. Today, let us linger on its first two words—'We believe'. We may see these as implying three things: an act of solidarity or bonding; an act of affirmation or saying 'yes'; and an act of commitment or determination.

'An act of solidarity.' There are other versions of our shared belief, and some of them begin with the word 'I'. This is obviously fine, in that nobody else can do your believing for you, any more than they can do your thinking or feeling for you. But this time the word chosen is 'We', which acknowledges that, although each of us is an individual, none of us is alone. This is very significant. At the heart of the Christian story is the claim that God creates us to be in a web of relationships. After all, each of us was born as a result of a relationship. It may have been a frail relationship, or a flawed one, but a relationship it was. In the same way, everything we know about the world, and all the skills we have, come to us as a result of an intricate set of relationships to which we don't necessarily advert, but which operate constantly to make up the human world at all. The language we use, the clothes we wear, the codes by which we know where we are in life—all of this is relational.

Christianity claims that God meets us, and blesses us, and gives us vitality in its many forms, by acting at the heart of these relationships. He is indeed 'my' God, but he is the true God of the true me, which is a me who is unbreakably associated with the others. The real 'me' is in part already part of the real 'we', and that is where God meets us—he has in fact no choice about that, since that is the way his own creation goes. When we say 'We' at the beginning of the Creed, we are consenting to ourselves, to the others, and to God's creative act.

What we say is, 'We believe'. The things we believe are spelled out after that; but let us notice here that this *is* an act of affirmation, *is* a saying 'yes'. And this too is important. It is important because there are many elements in our own culture which tend to suspend the saying of confident 'yes'-es. The famous film executive Samuel Goldwyn had a rather shaky command of the English language, and he is supposed to have said once, 'I'll give you a definite maybe'. We can all be inclined, whatever our age or experience, to say, much of the time, that we will give at best a 'definite maybe' to significant claims about life, about reality. The very fact that we have easy access to such an array of information and interpretation—on that great Web, for instance—can leave us hovering between one position and another. The Web is good, but it too can be a trap, in that sense. And in a similar way, universities are good—very good indeed, in my long and grateful experience of them—but they can also be an environment in which scepticism, suspended judgement, a 'definite maybe' to sizeable questions, can become another kind of trap.

When we say that we *do* believe the great headings of the Christian belief—we do believe, for instance, that a provident God works on our behalf every day, and always will; we do believe that God has come to be in our flesh and blood and in each of our relationships; we do believe that he will never desert our world—when we say this, we are taking a stand in the world, and about the world. We are claiming that we are prepared to do more than entertain some theories, or play some hunches, or toy with an interesting attitude to reality. We are saying that something is *so*—something exceedingly good, and something with large consequences for thought, and feeling, and action, and relationship.

Which brings me to the third implication of saying, 'We believe'. That implication is one of commitment, of determination. To 'believe' in this sense is to be 'tensed' as free persons, to be nerved morally and spiritually. It is to say that we are prepared to take the responsibility which flows from insight. Christianity is not only a view *of* the world, and of ourselves: it is a view *for* the world and ourselves. Creeds press towards deeds.

After all, in the history of Christianity, the various versions of the Creed which were formulated were themselves attempts to picture the deeds of God among us—creeds, in the first place, flowed from deeds, from divine deeds in a human world. The great 'credal' moment in the Christian year is in the midst of the Easter Vigil celebrations, where we hear readings from the Old and the New Testaments, readings which name God as creator, as rescuer, as blesser, as lover.

Creeds do not come from idleness, and when they are said with genuineness they do not indulge idleness. Our Creed, the one we are just about to say, names the major modes in which God has been good to us, and good for us: and it invites us, with some urgency, towards ways in which we can be good to one another and good for one another. Let us try to say it as if we do indeed mean it.

*Newman: March, 2000*

THE NICENE CREED

# One God, the Father Almighty

IN OUR CREED EACH SUNDAY, WE PLEDGE ourselves to believe in 'One God, the Father Almighty'. A very large library of books has been written about the elements in this phrase, and we have only minutes now: so I shall try to say only something very simple about it.

Several years ago, when the current Superior General of the Jesuits was visiting Australia, he was asked by someone from the press what he understood by the word, 'God'. To this he replied, 'He is the Father of our Lord Jesus Christ'. It was the right answer, and a good answer, because, as Christianity does, it lodged any understanding of God we have not in the abstract, much less in some aloof realm, but in relation to *our* Lord, and so in relation to us.

God is not ours for us to make what we will of him, like some god or goddess or godlet or godling of Greek or Roman mythology. God is supremely himself, and uniquely himself. But the God of Christianity is also the one who gives himself to us with all his heart, and acts on behalf of us with all his heart. He does not, as all of us do to some extent, have a divided heart: he is not, as we say, half-hearted in our regard. He is all at one, and he is all for us.

This is the absolutely important thing which Jesus the Lord came to bring home to his hearers. Certainly, the Jewish tradition already insisted on this, but our Lord not only preached it anew, but lived out its consequences with a unique coherence and integrity. If the final truth about all creation is not some faceless, though ingenious, complexity, but is truly what Dante famously calls 'the love that moves the sun and the other stars', if the final truth is a fathering and a fatherliness: then we will never be deserted. And if we are all the children of that one fatherly presence and power, then a first and final truth about us all is that we are indeed brothers and sisters to one another—are brothers and sisters now, and forever.

Dante's great phrase signals to us that we have to do here not only with a benign element in the cosmos, or a genial presence, but with power indeed—with what we might call the last word in power. God is not only a God of good intentions and benign disposition: God is the one who can make things happen, and does. 'The Father Almighty' is an expression which claims that at the very beginning of all we know or do not know, and at the very end of all we know or do not know, and continuously all the way through, God works lovingly on our behalf. In this chapel, many times over the decades since it was built, young couples have vowed to stand by each other 'in good times and in bad times, for richer or for poorer, in sickness and in health, until death'. That is the way God pledges himself to us, in creating us: and in his case, the pledge goes on past death into everlasting life.

Dante, the greatest of Christian poets, knew this, and would say our creed with us, word for word. But he was also a man of the world, more steeped in its anger and violence and betrayals than, please God, most of us are likely to be. He did not suppose that, in earthly experience, everything in the garden is rosy. In large degree, that is what his majestic book of a poem is about—about the blood on the roses: about exile, and fear, and loneliness. But he was committed to our belief that the God who fathers us gave us a divine Son to brother us—the one who would stand by us, and stand for us, come what may. In one of the Prefaces for the ordinary Sundays of the year, we thank the Father that he has indeed sent the Son, 'so that you might see and love in us what you see and love in Christ.' And in the end, the Father's greatest act of might, of power, is in his bringing about just that: in his bringing about that we are not only flesh and blood with his incarnate Son, but that we are, in God's eyes, Christ-like: that we have his Spirit.

This is amazing stuff. We do not have to think hard to find reasons to disbelieve it, or to doubt it—they thrust themselves at us, out of our experience, and any two-cent rattler on talk-back radio will back up those doubts. More than that, the Bible itself can be extremely eloquent about the fears and misgivings and disappointments which well up in any normal human heart—the Psalms are like this, very often, and the Book of Job is a tissue of such sentiments. Our Lord himself had no easy ride, early or late, in his life.

His last word, though, before death, is 'Father, it is into your hands that I yield up my spirit—the life within me'. It is absolutely essential to Christian belief that when he said this, he was heard, and was vindicated. His being raised from death and flooded, newly, with immortality, is the definitive sign that God was indeed 'the Father Almighty', and could never stop being just that One. And he is the One whom, in the words of the Mass in a little while, we dare to call 'Our Father'.

*Newman: March, 2000*

THE NICENE CREED

# *Maker of Heaven and Earth*

AT THE END OF THIS MASS, SOME OF US WILL WALK out onto Swanston Street, and as we approach our cars, will press the small device attached to the car-keys. Lights will flash for an instance, and we will know that the car is unlocked. Those of us who still have something of a child's heart will have a flicker of gratification at this. We used to believe in magic, once, and this looks like a sample of it.

Today we are thinking about those words of the Creed which proclaim God as 'Maker of heaven and earth: of all that is, seen and unseen'. That is the God who makes possible, and makes real, Swanston Street itself, and the car, and the unlocking device, and the flash of light, and the mind that recognizes the light, and the pleasure we have when we see it. He believes in magic still—he always has believed in it—and magic's great coup is existence itself.

'Maker of heaven and earth' we say: and we say of that God that he makes everything out of nothing. Nobody can imagine this, since 'nothing' is not something very diluted, or very spiritual, or even very abstract: it's nothing at all, it's not there. To say that God makes you and me and Swanston Street out of nothing means that the power he deploys is so great that nothing at all is needed for him to work on. As I say, we can't imagine this—our imaginations can't get any traction on it. But there are two notions, or insights, with which we can perhaps do something.

# Bread for the Journey

The first of these is that to make is always in some degree to *shape*. Out of the raw metal, plastic, glass and fabric comes a shaped thing called the car on Swanston Street; out of elements animal, mineral and vegetable, come all the shaped things called meals on Lygon Street. Something which was not fashioned in any way, was not shaped in any way, would not be a thing at all. We can do the fashioning with our hands—as with car and the food: or with our minds—as with the words and thoughts I am using, and you are recognizing, at this moment. Either way, we are evading chaos: we are backing meaning; we are, as we say, making something real; we are *getting* real.

The God in whom we believe is, through and through, the God of the real; he is the evader of chaos, the backer of meaning. He is the God of harmony, of fit, of coherence. He is a maker indeed. I am reminded of the fact that, in more than one language, the word for poetry is 'something made', and the word for a poet is 'a maker'. Poetry, like all of the arts, has to do with identifying and celebrating significance—of finding currents in the flow of events, shape in the midst of sprawl, pattern on the field of boundless possibility. You will indulge me if I see God as being, in that sense, the poet of the cosmos: the poet-shaper of planets and stars, but the poet-shaper of our minds and hearts too. 'Maker of heaven and earth, of all that is, seen and unseen.'

There is one other thing we can say, and I have implied it already. It is this. Although, in Lent, we do not say the 'Glory to God in the Highest' at the Sunday Masses, there is a sense in which the Creed itself is a song of celebration. Because when we acknowledge God as the fashioner of all that is, seen and unseen—of the car on Swanston Street and of our minds that know it—we acknowledge too what we might call his artistic drive or thrust. Ultimately, that artistic drive is one of delight.

People can make some pretty odd poems, paintings, films, plays and so on, and some pretty grim ones: but the artist's primal drive is towards saying 'yes!' It is a drive not only against meaninglessness, but towards delight, towards joy. Shakespeare wrote *King Lear* not simply to name distress of various kinds, but in pursuit of the pleas-

## Creed

ure of insight, and of pleasure in a language in which truth can be told greatly and well. God makes the world, makes us, out of an exultancy in a language of significance and harmony—a language which, in fact, he himself is. All of his making is a form of celebration.

Which is not to say, simply, that everything in the garden is lovely. We are not in a garden, and plenty of things are not lovely—the crucifix at every altar itself reminds us of that. But we will make no sense at all of the crucifix, or of our being here today, or in the end of our being in the world itself, unless we come back again and again to the God who says 'yes!' to what is. That is the God to whom we ourselves say 'yes': and the Mass is a major way of doing just that.

*Newman: March, 2000*

> THE NICENE CREED

# Jesus Christ, His Only Son, Our Lord

I HAVE SAID BEFORE THAT 'CREEDS PRESS TOWARDS deeds', and this is so not only in the sense that what we do should be of a piece with what we believe, but in the sense that everything we believe about God is a belief about God alive—God in action for us, and for our salvation.

This is true of the phrase in which we say that Jesus Christ, God's own Son, is our Lord. In St John's Gospel, that Lord tells us that 'the Father, who is the source of life, has made the Son the source of life'. Like Father, like Son: it is in the words and deeds of Jesus, the Commissioned One, that we know what the Father has to say of himself, and know what he does—know how he goes.

Our Lord, when he spells out who he is for us, says that he is 'the Way'. This means that he is our path, our route, to God the origin of all: it also means that he is God's 'route' to us. Perhaps we can think of it like this: when we learn 'the way' of doing something—the way to drive a car, or to cook, or to relate deeply to anyone else—that 'way' is an involvement, is a kind of entry, is a bonding. Jesus the Lord is God's 'way' of bonding with us, and is our 'way' of bonding with God.

What this means in practice is that when we are gathered into the rhythm of hearing the words of Jesus and chiming in with the generous deeds of Jesus, we are being attuned to God himself. In some real measure, it can be said then, of us too, 'like Father, like son', or 'like Father, like daughter'.

## Creed

The good news about this is that we do not have to hunt for God through forests of abstraction, or to wait for visionary moments; for our Lord assures us many times that where we find other men and women we are finding him, who is indeed the trace, the echo, of the Father. The bad news—or at least the challenging news—is that if we would indeed be attuned to God, and if we are not to live lives of fantasy, we have each day to accept the challenge to find the trace of Christ in the people we know. To say that we believe in Jesus Christ our Lord, who is God's only Son and his last word, is to say that we will never give up on trying to love those whom God loves into being, and into being the siblings of Christ.

If we are frank, this can seem an improbable agenda, when we look at some of 'the others', and when we look at ourselves. But in fact each Eucharist, and so this Eucharist, says 'thank God' to God's own promise that he, and his dear Son, and their shared Spirit, are at work night and day to school us in the loving to which we are called. There *is* a way for each of us, however dismayed or dejected or disarrayed we may be, a way for each of us to rise to courage and generosity, a way for today—and that is truly Christ's way, is truly Christ *being* our way. And he is never more 'Our Lord' than when he is being that way.

What do I mean by this? Let me illustrate it by mentioning something which some of you have heard me say before. Our modern English word 'Lord' comes from two Anglo-Saxon or Old English words of a thousand and more years ago: the word for a loaf of bread—'hlaf'—and the word for a keeper—'ward'. The idea was that you gave your allegiance to the one who gave you your food. It was the gift of food that was the very mark of lordship—you were devoted to him because he was devoted to you. The lord was the bread-man, and the bread, in all its simplicity, spoke eloquently of the lord's dedication, even his love.

You can see why I would be pleased by this scrap of etymology. Jesus Christ is the nourishment of our deepest life, of our most authentic love, and he is also the giver of that nourishment. 'Take this, it is my body', he says, giving nothing less than himself. From the first, the Church has celebrated that very fact, in the Eucharist.

But, as we can see from the New Testament, even the first generation of Christians needed to be reminded that God's gift of himself is not a private dole, given to one man or woman without reference to others. They had to be reminded, as surely we do too, that the Bread-giver gives himself, and his life, for all the world. He gives as he is, and he is in solidarity. That is his way, he is that way: and year by year, it must become our way too.

*Newman: April, 2000*

THE NICENE
CREED

# *For Our Salvation, Came Down from Heaven*

OF ALL THE ELEMENTS IN THE CREED, ONE OF THE hardest for us to take in may be the expression, 'It was for us, and for our salvation, that [Jesus Christ] came down from heaven'. I am not thinking so much of the celestial mechanics implied in these words—the grand descent from the grandly remote place. I am thinking, rather, of the claim that the living God, the envisager of all, and the fashioner of all, and the director of all, embroils Himself in all. After all, even though we are glad when expert figures in our lives—like teachers or doctors or lawyers or airline pilots—can feel for us and even 'identify with' us, in the end we know, and we accept, that they should have a certain distance from us: a certain expertise, a certain untouchability. How could they help us, if they were too much like us?

The truly disconcerting thing about Christianity is its claim that, in the person of Jesus Christ, the gap between the zone of humanity and the zone of divinity is annihilated. It insists that Jesus is neither a god rigged-up as a human being nor a human being rigged-up as a god. It insists, by contrast, on this: that because Jesus is, truly, to his fingertips, and to his heart's innermost chamber, and to the last point of his memories and his hopes and his dreams, absolutely human *and* absolutely divine, then the drama of the cosmos is a drama of divinity marrying humanity. This is shocking. It is, as people sometimes say, 'a shocking state of affairs'. If we do not find

Christianity shocking, this just means that we have not understood what it really is.

Why does God do this—not 'did', 'does', because that wedding goes on being reiterated, reenacted, every day? We can be sure of this: it is not just a virtuoso performance, an astounding show. The Irish musical group, The Chieftans, have often played certain pieces much faster than others do, and when they are asked why they do this, they say, 'Because we can'. God does not knit himself into our flesh and blood just because he can; he does it so that we can be bettered, from the inside, as to all our human frailties: our taking to dead ends on life's journey; our fieryness and our icyness towards one another; our indifference towards him, who is our source and our goal; our pathological scornings of ourselves. All deep healing has to be healing from the inside, outwards: God-in-our-flesh heals us from the inside, outwards.

When the incidentals of the Mass were modelled differently from those of the present, and when all was in Latin, the congregation heard near the end the words, '*Et Verbum caro factum est*'—which translates as, 'And the Word was made flesh': but which has also been translated, accurately, as 'The Word-Flesh is a fact'. And this is as much as to say that God blends what he has to say of *himself* with what he has to say of *us*. It is to say that God can never get us out of his mind, or off his agenda. There is no way that the Father can think lovingly of his Son without thinking lovingly of us. We are part of anything he has, importantly, to say: we are part of the burden of his essential song.

Which does not mean that nothing is called for as action, nothing is to be animated, nothing is to be changed. When those we love are awry, we want very much for them to change, and to be changed: when they are like parodies of themselves, we want their true image, their true face, to show itself. Love hungers for authenticity: it is thirsty for the genuineness which it can love all the more. So when we attest our belief that the Word has been made flesh, our flesh, we must by the same logic acknowledge our own need to grow, and to change. What we must never fear, though, is that we we will have to do this by ourselves. In God's idiom, in God's vocabulary, and by God's providence, 'by ourselves' does not mean anything at all.

*Newman: May, 2000*

THE NICENE
CREED

# On Saying Yes

I WANT TO SAY A FEW WORDS ABOUT AN ALL-important matter—about *the* all-important matter. I am speaking about that moment in the Creed in which we acknowledge that the Son of God, 'by the power of the Holy Spirit, took flesh from the Virgin Mary', and so became one of us. I am the first to acknowledge that, in the face of this mysterious reality, either we could talk for ever, or we could find ourselves wordless. Still, when we call God's living Presence among us 'the Word', we are surely conceding that he thinks some words appropriate, however limping: and so I shall limp along, a little.

Several years ago, when the celebrated Irish poet Seamus Heaney was visiting Australia, he described himself, in the course of an interview, as a 'yes-man'. By this, he did not mean that he is someone whose policy it is to bow and scrape, or someone who can merely charm the birds out of the trees, and charm misgiving out of the mouth. He meant, on the contrary, that even though life at large, and particular histories, can incline any of us to be spitters-out of scepticism and cynicism—as Heaney has charted eloquently in his writings—he is still one to say 'yes' to life, 'yes' to its worth, to its possibilities, to its generating further vitalities. To be, in that sense, a 'yes'-man, a 'yes'-woman, requires a mustering of moral resolves, and a scanning of memories, and a bracing for future possibilities. 'Yes' can be not only the best, but the hardest, of words to say.

## Bread for the Journey

And in that lies its relevance to our little formulation for today—the one about the Spirit's power and Mary's consent. There are countless pictures of the angel's announcing to Mary her critical moment for yes-saying. Among them is a very beautiful painting, now to be found in the National Gallery of the United States, in Washington. In that painting, by Van Eyck, the angel Gabriel is suitably splendid, and Mary is suitably receptive. But a key detail in it all is the floor, whose tiles represent various occasions of stress, and sometimes of convulsion, in the history of her people. It is as if when the angel comes to her, the ground stirs.

In Van Eyck's interpretation, the moment of Mary's 'yes'-saying does not occur without complexity. In the convention of the time, his painting shows the radiation of the Holy Spirit into her person: the golden gift of the Christ with whom she becomes pregnant is clearly a sublime accomplishment, beyond any human power to bring about. But that floor beneath her feet will not go away, the floor which has all the stir, and dissatisfaction, and surprise, of history inscribed upon it.

And this is the Mary who is named in every Mass, who is invoked in every Rosary, who is being called upon by thousands of people, perhaps millions, as I speak. Any time you have said the 'Hail, Mary', you have been quoting the angel of that radiant moment, and you have in effect been joining in with Mary's 'yes' to God's 'yes' to us. At that same time, while you said the prayer, you have named the condition in which, and for which, that double 'yes' was said; for our prayer ends with the words, 'pray for us sinners, now and at the hour of our death'.

That we are sinners does not need much demonstrating—a quick scan of the last day or so will bring up misgivings, warranted misgivings, in most of us. But I think that at the heart of our sinfulness, over that last day or so, lies a general reluctance to say 'yes' to the invitation to 'life and fuller life'. Our sins do not flow from lavishness of spirit: they flow from our huddling in the cave of fear, away from the great plains of God's creativity, his largesse. To ask Mary that she pray for us sinners is to ask that she help us walk with freed hearts, with resolute spirits.

*Creed*

And to ask her that she pray for us 'now and at the hour of our death' is to be realistic about how we are, and who, and where. None of us is a titan: all of us live by the clock and the calendar; and whether we are young or old—as the memorial tree outside this chapel for Ryan Draper may remind us\*—we all have one absolute, unknown deadline in life. In the midst of all this frailty, and in the midst of all the foolishness which so often goes along with it, we still turn, very sensibly, to the woman who, when she was younger than almost anyone here today, said 'yes' to God, a 'yes' for us all. She did this, not because it was unavoidable, or because it was theatrically interesting, or because it seemed a good idea at the time: she did it, as the Holy Spirit prompted it, 'for us and for our salvation.' Which means that we have a permanent claim on her help—as indeed we have on that Spirit who helps us, every day of our lives, to say 'yes' to him.

*Newman: May, 2000*

\* *Ryan Draper was a first-year student who was killed in a car accident.*

**THE NICENE CREED**

# *For Our Sake, Crucified Under Pontius Pilate*

WHEN I WAS A YOUNG MAN, A SARDONIC STUDENT gave me a gift. It was a candle, a globular candle, modelled in the form of the head of the Victorian Premier, Henry Bolte. I suppose that Mr Bolte's mother loved Mr Bolte, and I know that God did and does: but others were known to have problems with him. He did various kinds of good: he also presided over the execution of the last person to be hanged in this state. His head, which was pudgy and bulging, was well calculated to melt, vividly, if it were done in wax, when the wick was lit. And so it did, many times, when various people lit his effigy, in those long-ago days.

In a sense, this is what has happened to the name, and the notion, of Pontius Pilate: as a person, he has melted away into nonentity, and yet, as a figure, he has remained vivid. One sensitive and extremely industrious writer, Ann Wroe, has written a large book about the ways in which Pilate has cropped up, in memory and legend and imagination, over the centuries. There is something deeply ironic about the fact that this judge and sentencer of Jesus Christ, a Roman who is otherwise of little historical consequence, should have become one of the half-dozen most frequently-mentioned individuals in the history of the western world. There they are, the two of them, as at the first Station of the Cross—the doomer and the doomed, right at the historical fulcrum of our salvation.

## Creed

For all the later vilification of Pilate, we know nothing of his eternal fortunes: for all I know, he was eventually embraced in heaven by the taciturn Man whom he sentenced to death. What we can say is that when we think of our Lord's crucifixion, we are thinking of something which was as spiked into time as his wrists and feet were spiked into the wood. The Gospel, referring to the birth of Jesus, as of his death, insists on fixing it in terms of time, of place, and of authority. After all, these are the terms in which we all live: calendars and clocks give us our scale; atlases and street-maps bound our spot; gazettes and formal bulletins tell us what we may, and may not, do. There is, in Switzerland, a Mount Pilatus, named after Pilate: and a Mount Pilatus, compounding when, and where, and what, looms in its shadowy way over all our lives.

My brothers and sisters, I think that we will understand nothing about the actuality of Jesus, his actuality then and his actuality now, until it dawns on us that he is like the cry of the cock which agitated the evasive Peter, or the cry of the alarming clock which agitates us, whether or not we now want it, in our sleep. Christ's is a call, a clamour, in the night of time, of history: a call, a clamour, in our own night, in our own history. If he is bigger than time, and becomes a myth—something like the mythicized Henry Bolte of the candle, or the mythicized Pontius Pilate of the mountain. he is bigger than time because he is *imperative,* is emphatic, at each moment. An American poet I knew a little, Howard Nemerov, never I think himself a believer, but with the sting of Jewish atheism in him, wrote once of individual moments, '... it is now/ In the saddle of space, where argosies of dust/ Sail outward blazing, and the mind of God,/ The flash across the gap of being, thinks/ In the instant absence of forever: now.' God does not know deferral: God does not know decay: God's tall spike of promise, and challenge, and address, does indeed come down to the pinpoint of *now*.

Because my livelihood is made from the to-ing and fro-ing of words, I thought that I would check to see whether 'know' and 'now' have been bonded in their fortunes. It turns out that they have: and in a real sense it is true that we 'know' those things that 'now!' themselves to us. From time to time, all of us hate time. That odious term, 'deadlines', comes upon us, and how eloquent it is. We hate to be too late: we hate lack of convergence; we hate delay: we hate, in the end, the fact that, were we to be liberated from any and all other humiliations, we should still be strapped to time, as though to the hand of a clock. Whatever is, or fails to be, 'now', is deeply pungent for us. *Now is what we know.*

My dears, I am sorry that this is so. I like it no more than you do. And when, tomorrow, I go back to my human medley, where most people think that these claims, and all Christian claims, are nonsense, I would be glad to fall in with the notion that all of time, and all that happens in time, is expendable. But this I will never believe, since I am convinced that every moment of your time, and of my time, rings with the challenge of Christ's deed and call. Christ, and rightly, is called 'the Lord of time'. But this would be nonsense unless, sometimes at least, your next hour, and mine, could be uniquely precious.

*Newman: September, 2000*

THE NICENE
CREED

# *And Buried*

AT ONE POINT, IN THE FIFTEENTH CENTURY, THE great Italian artist Andrea Mantegna painted the dead Christ. Mantegna was a virtuoso, and he made the most of it. What we see is the body, feet-foremost, with the rest dwindling according to the newly-framed terms of perspective. The dead man is, if you like, being taken care of visually and conceptually. He is being monumentalised, as far as an immensely-skilled fellow human being can bring this about: he is joining the company of the illustrious dead.

But all this is the very opposite of what we naturally think of when we say of someone, as in the Creed we say of Christ, that they have been buried. Most if not all of us have, as we say, 'buried' those we love, and one day all of us will, please God, be 'buried' by those who love us. It makes no different if, for burial, we substitute cremation: joining the earth, we are joining a slower fire, but the outcome is the same. And what we are aware of, at least implicitly, is that burial does draw a thicker line under individual lives than pretty well anything else. Grand and all as the dead Christ may look in Mantegna's painting, the earth would despoil him, the fire would despoil him, as they would despoil anyone, of grandeur, great or small.

Earth, and fire. These terms may remind us that once upon a time the final elemental conditions of everything were thought to be fourfold: earth, fire, air, and water. The dead are in fact consigned, sometimes, to air, and to water too. And this, from a Christian perspective, is to the point. Because part of the brunt of what we say in the Creed is that the dead Christ, in being buried, is being exposed to the most formidable elemental forces of nature. Dying is bad: dead is worse: buried is worst, if we have in mind the very sapping of identity. It is as if the stone rolled to encase the dead man is also something to erase him. 'Buried' says, in effect, 'given over to obliteration by nature's forces'. 'Buried' says, 'soon there will be no remnant, even, to which to say goodbye'.

Burial makes us sick at heart, and well it might. We toss a handful of earth upon the coffins of those we have loved, and our mortal hands quail at the gesture. And this is why our present article of the Creed is so momentous. When, each Sunday, we move at a brisk clip from one point to another in that Creed, we dip, so to speak, into the allusion to the crucifixion and the death of our Lord, and, with understandable relief, we then lift to attest his resurrection. This is all to the good: this is how it should be. As Christians, we are all meant to be so many lamps, so many candles: to ignite hope is our business—just as, for those of us who are members of this College, that ignition is also our motto. But what I would urge upon your attention, as upon my own, is, that to mention the *burying*, and to imply its consequences, and then to retort against those consequences, is not only crucial for Christian belief, but is also critical for our own attitudes to our own lives.

The poet W. H. Auden wrote once of the death of Christ that he was 'as dead as we shall ever be': in other words—dead, outright. At that point, we assume that nature's processes will be all-commanding: will dominate, first and last. But if we believe in the resurrection of Christ, we believe in a rebuttal of those processes. *We believe in a retort against inevitability.* Every time we come to Mass, we conduct, as it were, a mini-Easter: we meet because he rose. And, correspondingly, we are summoned to believe that there is a difference between the ineluctable, or the fated, on the one hand, and the providential or the resurrectional on the other. The Christ who was consigned, in haste, and with grief and alarm, by those who got his wrecked body down from the cross, to the tomb, that darkly private place, was also the one of whom the later natural processes could not take command. The earth, and the air, and the fire, and the water, had in effect to stand back. Paintings show soldiers reeling: but we are talking about nature reeling. In the face of fate's claims, resurrection prevailed.

Every time we come to Mass, we re-dramatise, we re-enact, this belief, this truth, this fact. And to do it ritually is a very good thing—perhaps a better thing than you or I can ever find words for. But it seems to me that, sometimes at least, the ritual's eloquence should lodge in our own hearts as policy. If we do indeed believe that the resurrection of the Lord is a retort against inevitability, then surely this should provoke us to resoluteness against all the heart-draining bogus 'absolutes' of our daily, or weekly, lives. The preferred lodging of the devil, the cool, sterile and lethal place into which he wishes to lure us, is that tomb of hopelessness in which, so he says, nothing can be altered for the better, and we, therefore, need not try to change and grow. Against all that, our Lord retorted, by rising. Once upon a time, at baptism, each of us was plunged into that Life of Christ. Forget about the earth, and the air, and the fire, if you like: but remember the water—and take some when you go out.

*Newman: September, 2000*

**THE NICENE CREED**

# *He Rose*

DURING THE SECOND WORLD WAR, IN AT LEAST some of the countries occupied by the Nazi forces, it was a practice to whistle or to hum the first four notes of one of Beethoven's most familiar works; and the reason for this is that they were also, in Morse Code, the notes which signified the letter 'V': and that, of course, stood for 'Victory.' It continued to stand for victory, whatever conquests were achieved by Hitler's troops, and whatever atrocities were perpetrated by them, and whatever demoralization all this brought about among those who were opposed to him. This slender, brief signal, which met the ear for only a second or two, defied all the vileness of Nazism, and piped good news, however briefly.

Every time we say the Creed, we are in effect tapping out that letter 'V', for victory. It is true that we are not, thank God, under Nazi oppression, any more than we are under the heel of those Stalinist killers who murdered more than the Nazis did. But we are, even the most dashing and gifted and vivacious of us, living in the milieu of mortality; and the older we get, the more thoroughly we inhabit that milieu. We inhabit it not simply in the sense that our organisms wind down and ready themselves to check out: but in the sense that, cumulatively, we become aware of, and then we remember, the afflictions of our country and our world. A dear friend of mine, who was buried from this chapel almost exactly a year ago, was

## Creed

the first British officer into one of the main German concentration camps: any time he thought of his past—and he could think of having been Laurence Olivier's junior at school, for instance—the filth and infamy of that moment would bid for his attention. More banally, this is my tenth year in this College, and the spot where I live gives me a clear, uncomplicated view of the Melbourne General Cemetery, whose nearest monuments are there for the seeing whenever I blink myself into consciousness each morning. Living at Newman can be, at least for some of us, a school of realism in the most elemental of senses. It might, therefore, point to a folding up of aspiration, a closing down of expectations.

And yet, my dears, and yet ... Think, for a moment, not of the fine, broad, and thoroughly dead pews in which you are all sitting at the moment, but of what is at the end of each of the pews. The wood issues, there, in the statuette of a human being. It is as if this dark tissue has, after all, flowered. Out of the static, the pragmatic, and the finally expendable, a symbolized self blossoms. Earlier in the history of Christian symbolism, people used not sound-cues (as with the Beethoven/Morse-Code for victory) but visual-cues (as with a fish to stand for Christ). I don't know whether anyone used a combination of the seen and the heard, so that a rose might stand for the One who rose: but if they haven't, now we have. Christ, rising, flowered out of what seemed as sterile as the seats you are sitting on.

This is a Sunday, which is to say a festival of resurrection. We should pray every day: indeed, as our Lord says, challengingly, we should pray always: but this is the day on which, in the long and primal tradition of the Church, we quite deliberately celebrate the fact that the Lord's vitality could not be staunched even by death itself. And we celebrate this fact not simply as gazers or gapers at the performance of a star—Christ is our saviour, but he is not our beguiler—but as the ones for whose sake all this is happening. There is absolutely no element in our Lord's achievement, not even the slightest, which is devoted to prestige. In a real sense, he is a totally fameless one, if by fame we understand something which sheds a blaze of embraced applause upon the person in question. True, and happily, we recite, in the 'Gloria', the glories of the God who made us: but all of those glories are totally unselfish. Not only in this life, but in the life to come, we shall be finding ways to rejoice in God as the lavisher, as the lavish one.

The real Jesus, who was really done to death, really rose. And what is meant by 'rose' is not mere recovery—because where would that leave him, or us, or anyone? His rising means at least that, though there be cemeteries, and though there be Belsens and Buchenwalds, and though there be deaths of the innocent young, and deaths of good endeavours, and deaths of the heart—many and many of them—the realm of death itself has been made obsolete. It is withering on the vine, and the dark vine itself is withering. The age of the Rose is come instead: and all of us, for all the thorns of the Rose's age, must pick our way to the One who gives it life.

*Newman: September, 2000*

THE NICENE
CREED

*Ascended to the Right Hand of the Father*

RECENTLY, I WAS LOANED A BOOK BY A PROFESSOR of this University, a professor of some gravity and celebrity. The book is called, *The Larrikin Streak: Australian Writers Look at the Legend*. Some of its flavour may be captured from one detail which it records: 'During the 1930s, at a Test match, an English cricketer in the field was swatting at flies. A spectator shouted, "Leave our flies alone, you Pommy bastard!"'

It was indeed a larrikin moment—in it spiritedness, its feeling for the farcical, its provincial enthusiasm, its aggression, and its element of outburst or outcry. And I hope that you will not think me irreverent if I say that it has something to teach us about our Lord's keeping faith with us, perpetually. I think that it sheds some light on the notion of that Lord's being, as we say in the Creed, 'ascended to the right hand of the Father'.

For our Lord was himself spirited: and, as his sayings often testify, had a feeling for the farcical in life. He had a provincial enthusiasm, and his enthusiasm was all for the tiny province of Earth, a galactic pinprick for which nonetheless he lived and died and rose. He was intensely aggressive—was at war with all that was humanly or divinely odious, tainted at heart, poisonous for men, or women, or children: and in fact, he died at war, and of his war. And to round out the account, he was emphatically someone of outburst and outcry—

outcry sometimes at hypocrisy or cruelty or predatoriness or rampant narcissism, but sometimes on behalf of those things and experiences which we are all too prone to cherish too little. He is the singer of the flowers, even in their frailty: of generosity, even when shadowed by misery: of courage, even doomed courage: of fidelity, in the midst of all that mocks fidelity. And by those criteria, he is the larrikin Son of God. He is of us: he is for us: and at the same time, he is the one with whom we must hope to be matched.

This is the one of whom we say in the Creed that he 'ascended into heaven, and is seated at the right hand of the Father'. There are many splendid paintings of such a scene. The gold of mosaics, the brilliantly eloquent oils of one master after another—these attest the eternal grandeur of the risen and ascended Christ. He sits, in the place of honour, next to the Father who commissioned him for the work of our salvation. The men—and they were mostly men—who made such paintings had their own sense of values and priorities when they went about their work. Often, they thought imperially, and it was an imperial Father who was portrayed, attended by an imperial Son—the one who, through blood, sweat and tears, had indeed come into his own Kingdom. Who am I to deny a precious truth in such a view of things? After all, every year we celebrate, and properly celebrate, a festival of Christ the Universal King; and that feast is, in effect, a spelling out of the risen Lord's being, once and for all, in creative and saving concert with the One who fathers him.

But it is also true that we know of the Father what we see in the Son, and via the Son. Jesus himself is, in effect, the voiceprint, the heartprint, the selfprint, of his Father. And what we see in the gospels is the faithful Son who is also the faithful reproduction of his Father, in word and deed. The vivacity of Christ, the zest of Christ, the anger of Christ against deathliness, the refusal to take seriously the very many things which are not serious, the instinctive readiness of Christ to be plainspoken about the bad and to be lyrical about the good—this style, perhaps 'larrikin', is what the good Son learns from the best of Fathers.

We know that these were the ways of Jesus the Lord because we, the Church, witnessed him behaving in this fashion, being in this fashion, when he was palpably among us. And surely we may say that, having been done to death in large measure just because he was like that, and having been raised from the dead precisely because his loving fidelity did not falter although it had to go just those ways, he continues to cut that figure at the right hand of the Father. For Jesus Christ, to keep faith with his Father was, identically, to keep faith with us. And that one 'way'—a name or slogan he chose for himself after all—that one 'way' was never a way of cruising serenely, imperially, over the surface of human events, any more than it was a way simply of being engulphed, passively, by them. The Christ of the Gospels is at once receptive, responsive, and full of initiative. He is, accordingly, both a splendid example and a deeply provocative nuisance to anyone who wishes to engage in an 'imitation of Christ.'

We are all stuck with being 'imitators of Christ': there is simply no other way to be a Christian. And if we are really to catch his air, to have (if you don't like the notion of a larrikin streak, at least) a christian streak, then we must reconcile ourselves to unsettlement: to swerves of the spirit: to a blend of resolution and deprivation: to deaths and risings, deaths and risings, so long as we live. For this was the style of the one who, for us and for our salvation, went deepest into disaster, and is now vindicated, eternally, by the Father of us all. It is a messy enough business: but it is also a blessed enough business: and it is the only business there is.

*Newman: September, 2000*

## THE NICENE CREED

# *To Judge the Living and the Dead*

YEARS AGO A BOOK WAS PUBLISHED WITH THE title, *The Best We Can Do*. It was an account of a murder trial, in England. The author's style was very precise, and quite without sensationalism. I have forgotten the name of defendant, and victim, and even of the author. What I do remember is the point of the title—which was that even so momentous a matter as trying someone for his or her life (as it then was), for the taking of another life, could still at best be only 'the best we can do.'

And the title has stuck in my mind mainly because it is universally applicable when it comes to human judgements of other persons—or of human judgements of our own persons, of ourselves. The judgements we arrive at are, at their very best, sometimes their agonizedly best, only the best we can do. When we are dealing with selves, we are dealing with mysteries. Every so often, nowadays, we get a scientific bulletin to say that the human brain is immensely more intricate than anything else known to us in the universe. I take it on faith that this is so, and am in no way surprised to hear it: for the brain is the mediator, or the vector, of the self, and nothing at all is in the hunt for intricacy, compared with the self. Show me a person—luminous if you like, transparent, open-handed—and I will show you a labyrinth. If there is one single thing upon which the intellectual and imaginative endeavours of the western world have agreed, for at least the last three thousand years, it is that this is so. All the honey of selfhood comes from the hive of enigma.

In practice, faced with this fact, we have indeed to do 'the best we can do.' For a while, God help me, I was in charge of the Jesuits in Australia—to whom I used to say, occasionally, that I judged none of them, but I appraised all of them. And for once I was right. I had to size them up according to achievement, and capacity, and initiative, and sociability, and all such good things—that is what being in charge means. But I could not—not just would not, but could not—put a single one of them into those scales of justice of which, in various religious traditions, some unearthly judge makes use to determine eternal worth. 'Do not judge, or you will be judged', says our Lord: or, in the equally stark words of Thomas Merton, 'Don't ask for justice—you might get it. Ask for mercy'. 'The best we can do' does not weigh so much as a fingernail, does not weigh the random hair on a comb, when we are talking of God's domain.

And the fact is that, sometimes to our disconcertment and penitence, and sometimes to our elation and celebration, all the deeds of the self are in God's domain. St Therese of Lisieux, one of the three Christian 'patrons' of Australia, meant precisely this when she spoke of her 'little way' of Christian fidelity. In terms of public performance she was no star—was barely a sputtering firework. But she knew, and others who lived with her gathered that she knew, that we live in a milieu of the momentous—that as human beings we stalk through the divine in our seemingly inconsiderable days. Early in the history of Christianity, in the Acts of the Apostles and in various of the Epistles, the first Christians bearing written witness to the Lord, and to his Father, and to their shared Spirit, insisted that God alone was their judge. It wasn't that they thought that they were too good for the human adjudicators: it was that they believed that only God could gauge the authenticity of those whom God had made his own.

Most people did not believe them when they said this—hence the contempt for Christianity, then as now: hence the persecution of Christians, then as—in various parts of the world—now. And it is also true that, again and again, we ourselves, who are privileged to call ourselves Christians, go on losing the plot, both about ourselves and about others. We lunge or lapse into 'worldly' estimations of our own behaviour, and lose our nerve when it comes to christian genuineness. On bad days, we bluff, and check to see where the social wind is blowing, and cringe before gratuitous authority, and swagger in the face of legitimate authority, and adopt all the social buffoonery habitual to those who suppose, and fear, that they are all on their own, and that, in the end, The Terminator will arrive.

All this is deeply understandable, like a baby's sucking its thumb: but, as with that practice, there is no future in it. And we also lose the plot when we assign, and consign, our fellow human beings, our fellow shadowed selves, to cages of our own choosing. It is as if, for a while, we really do suppose that appraisal could be judgement: that the flesh and spirit whom God chose to be his own could be cased and labelled, brightly or darkly: as if we could, spontaneously, make ourselves the surrogates of the God of heaven and earth. Shakespeare said once that this kind of behaviour 'makes the angels weep', and God alone knows what God must make of it.

So is there to be no judgement? Ah yes, there is. There is to be—and surely, day by day, already there is—a judgement of each of us, of all of us, according to how we have wished to keep faith with what the Lord God of heaven and earth has shown us, in his Son, as momentous, as critical, for our own lives. Much of this, please God, we will learn from the articulate Church: and much besides from the stirrings of the workaday Spirit of God, day by day. The ultimately disastrous thing would be for any of us to suppose that 'the best we can do' is to be determined by the flat, abolishing, dismissive tone which is the normal accent of the devil—a tone which has great play in contemporary Australia. Our Lord enjoined on us, once, that we should say 'yes' sometimes, meaning it, and 'no' at other times, also meaning it. These things, as we sometimes say, are matters of judgement. And indeed they are.

*Newman: November, 2000*

THE NICENE
CREED

# The Holy Ghost: Intimate and Ultimate

NAPOLEON BONAPARTE WAS REPELLANT IN various ways, but in his own line of country he was nobody's fool. Amongst the things he said about his generals was that he wanted them to have 'three o'clock in the morning courage'. What he was referring to was the fact that, at that hour of the day, most normal human beings feel reduced, perhaps exposed, and other things being equal, alone. Napoleon wanted those generals to be able to cope with the nakedness of spirit which is so often experienced at about that time.

Any of us can have a 'three o'clock in the morning' experience, at any time. And one reason this is so is that each of us is, truly, alone in the sense that each of us is a once-and-for-all person. Whatever of the devices of cloning, and other techno-biological contrivings, none of us replicates anyone else. Each of us is an Uluru, an Ayer's Rock, of the spirit. In the Book of Job, the rueful Job says, 'naked I came into the world, and naked I will go out of the world', and certainly he is right: but each of us also has, as a person, some of the astounding nakedness, the astounding originality, of the central figure in Boticelli's 'Birth of Venus'. The God who made us unveiled each of us as a singular event in the world, and on the world's behalf.

Now I know that there is a formidable array of romantic songs, and books, and films, and plays, which celebrate our singularity, and our immeasurable individual preciousness: but most of us, I suspect, find this hard to believe, at least when it comes to ourselves. Certainly, we find self-celebrating persons distasteful, and often farcical—though at least they have given the world the great gift of comic spectacle. And most of us, I would guess, at least after a certain age, feel that it is unbecoming to reflect very much upon ourselves: the bad news discovered might put us permanently into a 'three o'clock in the morning' disposition, and the good news might make us too cocky for our own good.

The point I want to make about the Holy Spirit, though, is that the Spirit has no such reservations or misgivings. The Holy Spirit, as is stressed at a number of critical points in the New Testament, is the Spirit of unflinching, and of unfailing, intimacy. The Holy Spirit actually is the inreaching of the Father and of the Son into our hearts, souls, spirits: as the Holy Spirit is, through and through, the inreaching of Father and Son, in love, into each other. The Holy Spirit is the blessing, and the endorsing, and the enabling, of our intimacy to ourselves: it is the Holy Spirit who makes us, in the fullest sense, 'personal', so that we need not wait, warily, on the fringes of ourselves; need not carry our own hearts as though they were ill-adjusted burdens; need not eye off 'the others' with the double distrust that they are different from us and that they are like us; need not be so many husks or shells to our own seeding yearnings. The Holy Spirit calls us home to ourselves. A celebrated Spanish philosopher, Ortega y Gasset, said once that we are 'locked outside ourselves.' The Holy Spirit is the key to the lock, the host of its opening, the blesser of arrival.

This same Holy Spirit, the tireless, patient, dynamic welcomer—the Intimate of intimacy—is also the Intimate of ultimacy. The One who offers to bring us home to our own hearts, and thus become hospitable to the hearts of others, also offers to bring us home to the heart of God. Paintings of the Annunciation to our Lady portray the Spirit as emissary, often as dove. The dove is eloquent as a symbol in part because it always implies an origin, a sender, a heartland which is also a homeland. And as such, by a kind of paradox, it calls us, who have been helped to enter a new-found-land of blessed selfhood, out of any mere nesting there, towards another new-found-land of blessed otherness—even to the depths of the blessed otherness of God's very heart.

And so it has come about, countless times, in the history of Christianity, that when individuals, or groupings of the believing community, have come home to themselves in challenged, converted and consoled prayer, they have become figures of outreach, of aspiration, and of confirmation for a yearning world. It is as if the Holy Spirit moves by the same dynamism as sustains the physical heart of each of us at this moment: we live at all, and we hope to flourish, only in virtue of a double movement, inwards and outwards, inwards and outwards, night and day, year by year.

Every image, every metaphor, we have for the divine is feeble beyond any words we have to name the feebleness. And yet the living God speaks to us in the language of fire and fountain, of bracing earth and lofting air. In this Eucharist, once again, we try to lay ourselves open to the eloquence of God, who is himself a Word. Surely, too, we should pray for one another, to be reassured that there is no least fragment of us, no tract of heart or cranny of spirit, which is not homeland for the Holy Spirit: and pray, too, that those animated hearts may reach towards the horizons which the Spirit shows us.

*Newman: November, 2000*

THE NICENE CREED

# Lane and Planet: Believing in the Church

MY DENTIST IS GOOD AT HIS CRAFT, AND IS ALSO A very pleasant man, but when I was driving home from seeing him recently, I was a little more wide-awake than usual—an experience you may recognize. On the way, I noticed that someone had been at work on a road-sign. Originally, it had said, 'Form one lane': but with the skilful addition of a couple of letters, it now said, 'Form one planet.' I formed one lane, and made it home, but the revised sign made me think.

We will say, in a few moments, that we believe in 'one, holy, Catholic and apostolic Church.' In doing so, we adopt the equivalent of a 'one-lane' formulation. We say, for one thing, that we do our believing not as isolated figures, nor in little clusters, but as participants in a community which reaches back to the apostles, and is offered to all the world, and is not at loggerheads with itself, and is blessed by the Spirit of all holiness with holiness itself. To attest, or confess, or chant this does significantly narrow the options—it makes for a kind of laneway in life. It means that we believe in the God who has fashioned and embraced a human community—with all its oddities, chanciness, fickleness and sin—a human community in and through which no one less than God can be found.

So being a sheer loner in life is ruled out—with all the advantages, and disadvantages, of such a policy. It means that we believe that the one Lord who died for us all, and the one Spirit aflame in us all, will work a unity which is sound, unstifling, and fertile. It means that the Christian community will be a milieu in which a humanity which is already blessed can find tokens of ampler, transforming, blessing, so that integrity ripens into sanctity. It means that we need never see ourselves as marooned in time or place, but may trace the presence, always and everywhere, of the Christ who is both the servant and the master of time and place.

To say and believe these things is, in effect, to be forming 'one lane'. To put it mildly, much of Australia does not live by this set of beliefs. Yet this is what we do believe, and this is why we are here at this Eucharist. But, to follow the lead of the adjuster of the road-sign, when we do form this one lane, when we do attest this ancient, still-fresh faith, we are also attempting to 'form one planet.'

I think of two 'planetary' expressions. The brilliantly grim Samuel Beckett, author of *Waiting for Godot*, has another play called *All That Fall*. In it, a vexed old woman, appealing for a simple bit of help from somebody else, bursts out with the words, 'Christ, what a planet!' This is a piece of black Irish joking: after all, it's not the planet's fault that we haven't made as much of a world of it as we could. But we know what she means: any local distress and disarray can, in effect, carry the trace of much wider distress and disarray. And if the speaker's cry is partly profane, it can also be heard as a warranted appeal to the One whom we believe to be the compassionate healer of all.

Which brings me to my other 'planetary' reference. Pedro Arrupe, the last Superior-General of the Jesuits, wrote an essay called *A Planet to Heal*. Perhaps the title was suggested by his having been, as a former student of medicine, at the scene of one of the two atomic bombs dropped in Japan. It was precisely as a follower of Christ in the Catholic church that Arrupe thought in planetary terms. He was grittily aware of life's many narrow ways: but he still sought to find, through the Church, the Christ whose planet this is—and the world drawn, gradually, by the Spirit, into fullest blessed being.

The path and the planet, the way and the world: we are no more allowed to choose between them than Christ himself was allowed to choose. Remembering that, may we take heart from the knowledge that we do not go alone.

*Newman: November, 2000*

THE NICENE CREED

# Standing Up Once and For All

OUR CREED CULMINATES WITH THE CLAIM THAT we 'look for the resurrection of the dead, and the life of the world to come'. To say the least, this sounds promising. What else can we say about it? One thing we can say for sure is that this is not just a question of the natural run of affairs. We are not talking, here, about something like the cycle of the seasons. A poet writes, 'If winter comes, can spring be far behind?', but no human death looks or feels like just a phase in a person's fortunes: it would be altogether too glib to say, 'When death comes, can resurrection be far behind?' No: the christian belief in the resurrection into immortality of our mortal selves hinges entirely on something which could never have been calculated from nature— namely, the resurrection of Christ himself.

We call Jesus Christ our 'Lord', indeed the Lord of creation: but he would not have been called that unless he was identified as the one who rose from death— rose, and brought in his train, brought with him by the same impetus, all of his sisters and brothers who would consent to go with him beyond deathliness into unquenchable vitality. Resurrection is, as it were, his leit-motif, his insignia, his ring of authenticity. When St Paul says, 'If Christ be not risen, our faith is in vain', he means as I take it not only that without resurrection there is no future for us, but that without resurrection all of a christian's enthusiasm about Christ himself is no more than zest about a shadow, however touching that shadow may be. And by contrast, for us to attest belief in resurrection is for us to say that Christ is so potently life-filled that a death undergone becomes a death rebutted. More: it is to say that we take this Lord at his word when he assures us that as he lives unquenchably, and as he bonds himself with us, we too may live unquenchably.

But this is indeed something believed in, not something seen. The phrase in the Creed says that we 'look to' or 'look for' the resurrection from death: none of us has been there. If we slept well last night, it was in part because, frail organisms that we are, we needed to do so: if we did not sleep well, we are probably feeling the effects: we are pilgrims of resurrection, not full participants in it. Still, just as there are traces of divine creativity in the world, there are signals of the presence of the Lord of resurrection. And let me point to one of them.

I have scarcely enough German to ask my way, but I do happen to know that in German what we call 'resurrection' is called, in effect, 'upstanding'. The Resurrection of the Lord is the 'upstanding' of the Lord. This is suggestive: because in English we have an idiom about 'standing up to be counted'. It means of course being ready to take responsibility— means, as we also say, taking a stand. And from the beginning of Christianity, one of the major things for which our Lord has been saluted was his readiness to stand up for what was right, and his readiness to stand beside those in need, and his readiness to stand for the daily living Presence of his Father. The figure he cuts in the gospels is that of such an 'upstander'— in fact, as uniquely that 'upstander.'

Even as I say this, though, you will be aware that the most familiar of all representations of Christ, the crucifix, has him upstanding indeed, but also as in the midst of dire vulnerability. The grandeur of his resoluteness, the boldness of his leadership— these have their starkest test in the midst of recurrent human need. Nobody knows the names of the two men crucified with him, even if one of them has had a traditional tag given to him: they stand, in effect, for the countless nameless millions of women and men who have gone, and go, and will go, through mortality's tests and tasks.

## Bread for the Journey

The Christ who came for them belonged with them, and belonged with them in their brokenness— as well as, elsewhere, with their eating and drinking and singing and dancing. The one who stands for us, stands for us through thick and thin. He is, so to speak, upstanding even in his downfall.

It is because he keeps faith with us in this way that he keeps faith with the Father who, we believe, never deserts us. Like Father, like Son: and tracing the fidelity of the Son, we may have some inkling of the fidelity of the Father. That Father, who rejoices in the Son's being 'upstanding' in the face of mortality, and in the face of the world's heartbreaking ills, 'raises him up' in vindication of his keeping faith with God and with humanity. In John's Gospel, Jesus tells his hearers that although he must go the mortal way in a dark time, he will still not leave them bereft. In effect, together with the bread and the wine, he puts on the table the promise of resurrection.

Here we are again, with the Lord's bread, the Lord's wine: and also with the Lord's promise of resurrection. The bread is shared, the wine is shared: and so is the promise. Any of us may become, perhaps in small ways but certainly in genuine ways, enacters of that promise. There will, today or tomorrow or next week, be moments when we can stand afresh for God, and stand afresh by one another. Then we shall truly be looking for the resurrection of the the dead, and for the life of the world to come.

*Newman: December, 2000*

# Indexes

## THE CHURCH'S YEAR

### Year A
Advent 1, 3
Advent 2, 7
Advent 3, 10
Advent 4, 13
Lent 1, 27
Lent 2, 30
Lent 2, 222
Lent 3, 33
Lent 5, 171
Easter 2, 48
Easter 3, 50
Easter 5, 53
Easter 5, 180
Ascension Day, 60
Trinity Sunday, 66
Corpus Christi, 69
Ord Sunday 2, 209
Ord Sunday 11, 225
Ord Sunday 14, 166
Ord Sunday 16, 191
Ord Sunday 17, 183
Ord Sunday 18, 174
Ord Sunday 19, 116
Ord Sunday 20, 219
Ord Sunday 22, 228
Ord Sunday 31, 135
Ord Sunday 32, 156
Ord Sunday 33, 189

### Year B
Lent 4, 35
Good Friday, 231
Passion Sunday, 198
Ord Sunday 3, 82

### Year C
Lent 3, 24
Lent 5, 37
Easter 3, 112
Easter 6, 56
Pentecost Sunday, 63
Christ, Universal King, 76

Ord Sunday 15, 203
Ord Sunday 17, 177
Ord Sunday 17, 212
Ord Sunday 20, 103
Ord Sunday 24, 206
Ord Sunday 28, 186
Ord Sunday 27, 90
Ord Sunday 29, 160
Ord Sunday 31, 214
Ord Sunday 32, 169

### General
All Saints, 73
Ash Wednesday, 24
Assumption of Mary, 79
Baptism of the Lord, 21
Christmas, 16
Easter Day, 45
Epiphany, 18
Good Friday, 43
Palm Sunday, 40

Year 1, Week 4, Wednesday, 147

## PEOPLE
Hacker, Jim, 135
Heaney, Seamus, 132
Keillor, Garrison, 60
O'Hearn, Dinny, 125
Ryan SJ, Noel, 128
Shakespeare, William, 139

## THEMES/ STORIES/ OCCASIONS
Abraham, 30, 222
angels, 194
Anzac Day, 97
Aquarius, 33
Ascension, the, 263
Australia Day, 94
autumn, 87
baptism, 21
belief, 272
blessings, 79
burning bush, the, 24
calling, 222
Canaanite Woman, the, 219
challenge, 27
community, 147
compassion, 177
conversion, 7
cross, 44
crowds, 63
daily bread, 112
death, 166, 257
decisions, 193
elections, 90
Eucharist, 183, 189
evil, 169
father, 212
fish, 112
gamble, 219
generosity, 228
Good Samaritan, the, 203
gratitude, 186
Halloween, 109
happiness, 13
hatred, 171
heaven, 13
Holy Spirit, the, 269
home, 180, 154
ideas, 56
Incarnation, the, 69, 249
Ireland, 156
irony, 3
judgement, 266
John the Baptist, 209
life, 36
life, new, 45, 166
Lord's Prayer, the, 214
longing, 160
love, 66, 153, 206, 240
marriage, 151
Mary, 251
Mother's Day, 106
New Adam, the, 231
Olympic Games, 99
ordinary time, 82

outsider, the, 214
palms, 40
Passion, the, 198
past, the, 132
peace, 10
play, 99
Pontius Pilate, 254
power, 90
prayer, 160, 177
pressure, 219
Prodigal Son, the, 206
race, the, 103
Resurrection, the, 260, 274
saints, 73
shepherd, 77, 225
sickness, 186
silence, 116
Thanksgiving, 152
Thomas, 48
university, the, 174
Valete, 118, 163
wisdom, 156, 163
words, 191
Zacchaeus, 214

## THE NICENE CREED

We Believe ..., 237
One God, the Father Almighty, 240
Maker of Heaven and Earth, 243
Jesus Christ, His Only Son, Our Lord, 246
For Our Salvation, Came Down from Heaven, 249
On Saying Yes, 251
For Our Sakes, Crucified under Pontius Pilate, 254
And Buried, 257
He Rose, 260
Ascended to the Right Hand of the Father, 263
To Judge the Living and the Dead, 266
The Holy Ghost: Intimate and Ultimate, 269
Lane and Planet: Believing in the Church, 272
Standing Up Once and for All, 274

www.ingramcontent.com/pod-product-compliance
Lightning Source LLC
Chambersburg PA
CBHW031100080526
44587CB00011B/753